PRAISE FOR *BRAINS ON FIRE*

"*Brains on Fire* succeeds at doing what so many other business books attempt: It provides a recipe for how every company can succeed. But the secret isn't in the latest tools, online communities, or campaign tactics. It's about passion, humanization, and common sense. And to prove that it's possible, *Brains on Fire* is filled with examples of organizations that have already done it."
  —Scott Monty
    Head of Social Media, Ford Motor Company

"*Brains on Fire* is loaded with great advice from a team of people who have repeatedly built successful movements, ranging from an anti-teen-smoking movement to a pro-city-parks movement. If you want to lead a movement, start with this book."
  —Dan Heath
    co-author of *Switch* and *Made to Stick*

"The world is both strange and small in a modern age, isn't it? There now seem to be a million fancy ways to reach and excite kindreds, like-mindeds, and customers anywhere in the world. A truly tantalizing notion. But for anyone who manages a business or a brand, the modern age has become increasingly difficult to decode in real time. More quickly than most of us would like to admit, the things we do to spread the message of our products, services, and causes devolve into dressed up versions of traditional strategies, a one-too-many controlled blast with a hat tip to an interactive tactic. It can be an unsatisfying exercise for all involved.

"Enter *Brains on Fire*. It isn't just a book or a company, it is a collection of real people, with souls and hearts and stories—oh, the stories!—able to offer real advice to anyone who wants to make a movement out of what they do all day. Put down your Powerpoints and ad campaigns, folks. This takes guts and faith and patience, but mostly it takes passion.

Not yours. Your *customers'*. *Brains on Fire* can help you find it, trust it, and gently blow on the ember until it ignites. It's not brand management, it's brand as transformation. You in? There's a truth that lies deep within the promise of this modern, digital world—that authentic leadership can be released from your customers, and their passion can be fanned into movements that change lives forever. *Brains on Fire* can help make it true for you. Buy the book."

—Ellen McGirt
Senior Writer, *Fast Company* magazine

"*Brains on Fire* has the ability to assemble a powerful team that speaks as one unit. This engaging book is all about how that team works, including love, hard work, shared passion, with a constant focus on the goal."

—Douglas J. Greenlaw
former Head of Sales and Promotional Marketing,
MTV Networks, New York

BRAINS ON FIRE

IGNITING POWERFUL, SUSTAINABLE,
WORD OF MOUTH MOVEMENTS

ROBBIN PHILLIPS, GREG CORDELL, GENO CHURCH, SPIKE JONES

WILEY

John Wiley & Sons, Inc.

Published by John Wiley & Sons, Inc., Hoboken, New Jersey.
Published simultaneously in Canada.

For general information on our other products and services or for technical support, please
contact our Customer Care Department within the United States at (800) 762-2974, outside the
United States at (317) 572-3993 or fax (317) 572-4002.

Wiley also publishes its books in a variety of electronic formats. Some content that appears in
print may not be available in electronic books. For more information about Wiley products,
visit our web site at www.wiley.com.

Library of Congress Cataloging-in-Publication Data:
Brains on fire : igniting powerful, sustainable, word of mouth movements / Robbin Phillips . . .
[et al.].
    p. cm.
  ISBN 978-0470-614181 (cloth); ISBN 978-0470-77053-5 (ebk); ISBN 978-0470-87226-0
(ebk); ISBN 978-0470-87227-7 (ebk)
  1. Word-of-mouth advertising.   2. Business referrals.   3. Consumer satisfaction.
I. Phillips, Robbin.
  HF5827.95.B73 2010
  659.13—dc22

                                                                    2010012324

Printed in the United States of America
10 9 8 7 6 5 4

This book is dedicated to our dear friend and founding partner, Mike Goot.

His outrageous, often obscene, yet infinitely kind and generous spirit is part of who we are.

It pushes us to be relentless in our pursuit of the truth, and to never surrender any possibility

that our efforts could help make the lives of those we touch more meaningful . . .

and a helluva lot more fun.

Contents

Acknowledgments

LOVE

Brains on Fire is not really a business book. It's a love story, a story about being famous for the people you love.

When I was first approached by Dan Ambrosio at John Wiley & Sons in August 2009 about writing a book, I instantly said, "Yes. *We* want to write a book."

When I say "we," I don't just mean the four authors you see listed on the cover. "We" represents an army of believers. It's the people who comment on our blog. It's the courageous clients we serve. It's their customers. It's everyone who sends us a resume or a love note. It's our employees and extended tribe. It's people who catch a vision and inquire about our services. It is all of us who are learning and changing the way we think about the work we do in the world.

However, there are some very special people whose contributions I need to mention by name.

Without the inspirational vision of Geno Church, this book would not exist. For sure, Geno is a thought leader in the word-of-mouth marketing world, but mostly he is one of the most honest and genuine human beings on the planet.

Greg Cordell is also a huge part of the heart and soul of Brains on Fire. We are inspired daily by his brilliant insight and wisdom. He has a deep and soulful understanding of the emotions that connect and unite people.

And then there are the clients and the people who call Brains on Fire home. I took on the task of interviewing many of our clients, employees, and advocates. It was life-changing. It was also a privilege to discuss ideas and lessons learned with so many bright and shiny people.

Greg Ramsey and Eric Whitlock visually bring our communities and movements to life on a daily basis. Eric caught a vision for the cover and ran with it. The artwork was not created by a single artist; rather, it is a collection of doodles from many of our kindred spirits who love to draw. (Frankly, we see the cover as a type of visual expression of a movement.)

And then there is Spike Jones. He's a talented writer who helped give our message one voice. He poured his heart into the assignment, and we are very grateful for his help.

We believe with all our heart and soul that Brains on Fire is a movement. Join us. Let's continue the conversation at brainsonfire.com/blog.

We're listening.

ox,
Robbin

We love our employees and extended tribe:

Brandy Amidon	Justin Gammon
Kim Banks	Matt Geib
Alexis Bass	Jen Goff
Neil Batavia	Mike Goot
Megan Byrd	Scott Gould
Geno Church	Cathy Harrison
Greg Cordell	Kim Hebert
Joe Dannelly	Heather Hough
Beth DeLong	Liza Jones
Eric Dodds	Shannon Kohn
Blair Enns	Samantha Lussier
Justine Foo	Logan Metcalfe

Acknowledgments

John Moore	Ron Reece
Robbin Phillips	Carol Reeves
Alison Quarles	Jack Welch
Greg Ramsey	Eric Whitlock

And our clients who graciously contributed to this story:

South Carolina DHEC & the RAGEers
Jamie Plesser & the Best Buy Mi11 Community
Jay Gillespie & the Fiskateers
Jim Martin & the Charleston Park Angels
Meg Smith & the IndieBound Community
Rob Morris & the Love146 Abolitionists
Sally McConnell & the America's Storytown Community

And our advocates who graciously contributed to this story:

Suzanne Fanning	Tonya Polydoroff
Chris Sandoval	Roger Dennis
Dan Heath	Ellen McGirt
Scott Monty	Francois Gossieaux
Dan Ambrosio and the team at John Wiley & Sons	

The many talented doodlers:

Chris Bradley	Eric Dodds
Alice Ratterree	Robbie Cobb
Kelly Johnson	Emory Cash
Megan Byrd	Bryan Martin
Robbin Phillips	Greg Ramsey
Greg Cordell	Justin Gammon
Shannon Kohn	Samantha Lussier
Eric Whitlock	Geno Church

It took an army of true believers . . .

Introduction

IT'S ABOUT PEOPLE, STUPID

Technology is a trap. A crutch. The shiny new object in the room. And while many people think it could be the answer to their prayers, we guarantee that it could also be your biggest detriment. A lot of companies that concentrate all their efforts in the area of technology seem to take the human element out of the equation. But the focus of business is not—and never should be—technology. Rather, it always has been, and always will be, about people. Living, breathing human beings with hopes and dreams, pet peeves, and a whole bunch of emotional baggage.

You will quickly discover that there are no social media how–tos in this book. There are no Twitter strategies, Facebook doodads, or MySpace thingamajigs. Sure, we'll touch on how technology can be used to create long-term, sustainable, profitable movements, but if you're looking for something completely technology-focused, then put down this book and go pick up the latest issue of *Wired*.

"It's about people. When it comes to technology, what's exciting and shiny today will be frickin' dead tomorrow."

Chris Sandoval – Member Experience Strategist
for a diversified financial services group serving
the Military community

You should also know that while there is a company out there in the world named Brains on Fire, this book isn't named after it. Nothing is named after our company. Brains on Fire is named after what we do—ignite passion within employees and customers—which is really where brains on fire happen. This book is therefore a celebration and tribute to the courage, vision, and enthusiasm of those companies and organizations we have had the honor to serve, because they are a true reflection of what Brains on Fire stands for. It is our hope that you can learn what our customers have taught us within these pages and, in doing so, open hearts and minds to new ways of strengthening the connections between people and companies. Our customers are Brains on Fire, their employees are Brains on Fire, and their customers are Brains on Fire. They are an extraordinary, energized, empowered community. Far from ordinary consumers or target markets, these amazing individuals have learned to channel their passion to bring about positive, real change in people's lives.

And so the torch gets passed. The love grows. And the world is better for it.

WHY SHOULD YOU CARE ABOUT THIS BOOK?

Because—as any number of books before this one told you—the landscape has changed. Before the rise of the Internet, companies could at least operate under the illusion that they controlled their messaging and could tell the public what to think about them. However, if you're a company today that still thinks that, then there's a lot more delusion than illusion going on.

It comes down to trust. And people don't trust your company; people trust people. People they know. People whose opinions and recommendations they seek out and have faith in.

People don't buy your company, product, or service first, they buy people first.

One question that we get a lot is "Well, how does this 'movement' thing apply to B2B?" We tell them that it's no longer a B2B, or even a B2C world; it's a P2P, as in person-to-person. Because your company is made up of people.

Another reason you should care about this book is because we live in a world where companies are fighting for their lives. No, don't worry; this isn't the part where we talk about the crappy economy or how you're a commodity or how the rise of the digital world has made your competition a lot fiercer. But when you're fighting for your life, you're a lot more willing to listen—to your customers and to your employees. Listen for advice on how to become a part of something that's bigger than you. That's where movements start: by listening.

WHAT IS A MOVEMENT?

No, we're not going to pull out the dictionary. We're just going to let you know that—for the purposes of what's ahead—we have developed our own working definition of what a movement is: A movement elevates and empowers people to unite a community around a common cause, passion, company, brand, or organization.

So let's take it a step further, since we're talking about sustainable movements here: A sustainable movement happens when customers and employees share their passion for a business or cause and become a self-perpetuating force for excitement, ideas, communication, and growth.

Your ultimate goal should be to ignite something so powerful that if your marketing and PR departments or, God forbid, even your entire company got hit by a bus, your fans would pick up the banner and march forward with it. Something like that takes many forms, and one might be your fans creating their own PR and marketing messages and picking up where you left off.

CAMPAIGNS VERSUS MOVEMENTS

Let's get something straight: We have come neither to praise traditional advertising, nor to bury it. It's not dead. It's not going away. So don't think that we're going to go into a tirade about how traditional advertising is broken, and you shouldn't be using it.

But allow us this sidebar: It's really intriguing to see, in 2010, the nostalgia that's being passed around about the way things used to be in the advertising world. The popular cable television drama *Mad Men* is all about the martini lunches and the thrill of the pitch back in the 1960s, Madison Avenue in its heyday. And there's something to be said about that: the good old days, trying to recapture the glory and thrill of the big, glitzy ad campaign.

Even today, the ad industry celebrates those fading stars of the old times, and when they do, they are acknowledging that those days are over. Sure, there are shining spots even in today's advertising. The ad rags call them out, and we all gather around and applaud, until we forget about it 20 minutes later because so few of them are memorable anymore. That brochure you designed is really just pretty trash, because that's where it's going to end up 10 seconds after someone looks at it. You're just creating more campaigns. And while campaigns try like hell, it's really hard to make a campaign into a movement. There's a big difference between the two.

Movement is also a word that's being thrown around a lot these days, especially by marketing folks. But if it feels, looks, and smells like an advertising campaign, then guess what: It's an ad campaign. Not a cultural movement or any other kind. Ads are a tool. Movements are the workshop. You have to understand the tactics before it makes any sense to implement. And when you start to look at your marketing challenges in the context of a movement, your world starts to change.

" If I had come through with a litany of tactics and things that we wanted to do, I would not have gotten very far."

Jamie Plesser – Best Buy
Consumer Marketing Manager

Jamie Plesser—who works in Marketing Strategy and Communication for retail giant Best Buy—said the following about the concept: An idea "has to be strategically sound and insight driven to get through our corporate organization. If I had come through with a litany of tactics and things that we wanted to do, I would not have gotten very far."

So to get in the right frame of mind, set the stage, and push you out of your comfort zone a bit, let's compare campaigns and movements.

CAMPAIGNS HAVE A BEGINNING AND AN END

Ah, the media buy. Pulling the plan together. Analyzing the data for the best demos. Looking at the ratings and placing your bet on where you'll get the most bang for your buck. You know what we're talking about, advertising types. Those typical TV media buys are four weeks long. And so you have an entire month to worry about whether you made the right decision with your client's money.

But let's back up even more than that, and say that your client has asked you to develop a new ad campaign. So your shop swings into action. The creative juices flow, the machine gets cranked up once again, and you pump out the concepts. Then, the thrill of the pitch. It's game day, and your A team brings out the big guns. The glamour. The oohs and aahs from the client (hopefully). You shoot and edit the TV spots, get the print ads ready for production, cut the radio spots. And then, the blessed launch day comes. Everything rolls out. Sometimes, even smoothly.

But sooner or later, your four weeks are up, and either you dump more cash into more media buys, or you go back to the drawing board and reinvent the wheel. We know that's not a bad proposition for ad agencies—since it just means more money in their pockets, not to mention the media buy markups—but do you have any idea what the average return on investment is for traditional advertising? Take a deep breath, because according to Copernicus Marketing Consulting and Research, the average ROI of TV advertising campaigns is 1–4 percent.

We don't know about you, but that's not exactly what we would call successful. Of course, there are shining spots out there that exceed that 4 percent and get really fantastic results, but you've got about the same chance at that as you do getting hit by a meteor.

So, to sum it up: Campaigns are designed to be finite. Start and stop. Beginning and end. Got it?

MOVEMENTS GO ON AS LONG AS KINDRED SPIRITS ARE INVOLVED

Different people use different words to describe a movement, but one overarching idea is always in place: A movement is sustainable. Rob Morris, president and co-founder of Love146—an organization you'll learn more about later that is out to end child-sex slavery and exploitation—defines a movement in the following way: "A movement is not something that happens in a year. It's something that continues to build [over time]."

> "A movement to me is
> something that is growing."
> **Scott Monty – Ford Motor Company,**
> **Head of Social Media**

Scott Monty, the head of social media for Ford Motor Company, agrees: "A movement is something that is growing. It's something [with which] people can identify and get behind, that kind of picks up its own momentum." Movements have a beginning. But the great ones—the powerful ones, the ones that end up changing the world and lives and even companies—go on and on and on. There is no end. Religion. Social change. Political change. You get the idea. There is no looming expiration date on a movement because it gains momentum as it goes. One kindred spirit attracts another, and another. All with different ideas and talents, but all for a common goal. So the groundswell begins. The roots take hold. It's the difference between a four-week ad buy and a 365-day-per-year engagement. Which one sounds better to you?

Another advantage that movements have over campaigns is that movements are people-powered. If you strip the humanity out of a movement, all you have is an empty shell. Empty shells don't move. For example, when you advertise on TV you're basically sponsoring the entertainment. So it's kind of like your message is sponsoring more messages. But how about sponsoring people's lives? That grows. A 30-second TV spot can't grow; it's dead after 30 seconds.

Creating versus Igniting Movements

It might be total semantics to a lot of folks, but we have a really hard time saying that you can "create" a movement. Because, really, can you create a movement? Or do you *ignite* them?

Think about it. When you create, you make something from nothing. You "cause something to come into being, as something unique that would not naturally evolve or that is not made by ordinary processes."

But something has to be there already to catch fire when you ignite. All the ingredients are there; they're just waiting. When it comes to movements, we're looking to ignite passion. Feelings. Connections. Sometimes it's dormant in people, and sometimes it's very active, but it already exists. It's just up to us to find it, throw kindling on it, and light the match. So while we might create tools and opportunities, creating a movement? Nope.

You can tell when someone tries to create a program, because if they have to create something out of nothing, we usually find that those folks are just creating something so people can talk about them. They're throwing a party and expecting people to show up. And that's a dead-on-arrival effort. That's not igniting the passion within. When you ignite someone's passion, you quickly find out that you must keep the conversation focused on them and their passion to fan those flames.

So change your mind-set. Don't create; ignite. And you'll see the differences. Not only in the way you approach your process, but in the results that it generates—like long-term sustainability—which makes your marketing dollar go so much further these days.

CAMPAIGNS ARE PART OF THE WAR VOCABULARY

In his book *The Culting of Brands,* author Douglas Atkin examines how the majority of brand managers (and ad agencies, for that matter) still speak in the language from the heyday of Madison Avenue way back in the 1960s. Atkin explains that this vocabulary stems from a command-control culture that imitates military speak. "They have campaigns, they target customers, they go for market domination, they launch an attack on competitors, they penetrate markets, and capture market share," Atkin reveals.

What a wake-up call. Do you really think people want to be targets? To have something launched to fight for their attention? No wonder the world is so wary of marketers! These terms are so ingrained in advertising publications, marketing classes, and our everyday lives that we don't even realize what we're saying and the mind frame in which we constantly put ourselves by using these words. This creates a daily situation wherein we—the marketers—are trying to defeat our customers. And what does that even mean? That they finally surrender to our constant attacks? That we succeed in brainwashing them and making them our captives? That we control their every move? Yeah, right.

MOVEMENTS ARE PART OF THE EVANGELIST VOCABULARY

While campaign words are rooted in conflict, movement words are rooted in drawing people together. Movements use words like *passion.* We talk about "kindred spirits" who raise their hands to become "evangelists." These people are "loud and proud" and provide others with "inspiration." And yes, there's even that big old scary *L* word: *love.* Oh, there are words we use in movements that aren't all mushy and lovey-dovey. Because movements also exist to fight an injustice. So yes, there are struggles and conflicts to be mindful of.

When we begin to change our vocabulary, we begin to change the way we think. Customers know that they're "targets," and nobody wants to be a target. They'll even go out of their way to avoid your message.

But maybe the problem is bigger than that. Since even words like *marketing* and *branding* mean so many different things to so many different people, maybe it's time to circle the wagons and change our own culture before we try to go out preaching it to potential clients. What if you didn't think about marketing at people and instead about talking with them? What if you didn't try to sell people something they didn't need so they can fit into your customer base and instead tried to figure out how you can fit into their lives in a useful, meaningful way?

Is that really a stretch? Some might think so. But if you can step back and think about actually adding value to people's lives, then a whole new world opens up. And you quit being a marketer . . . and start being a person.

CAMPAIGNS ARE DRY AND EMOTIONALLY DETACHED

Though estimates vary, it's been found that the average person is bombarded with somewhere between a few hundred and a few thousand advertising messages per day. Print. Outdoor. Online ads. TV. Radio. Text messages. Blah. Blah. Blah. And that's what 99.99999 percent of those ads are: blah. We're doing a great job as a society of blocking out those ads. Are there some we remember and talk about? Of course. But that percentage is so incredibly small compared with number of ads we're exposed to that the odds of your message sticking with someone are very, very slim. We're bored with them. They are something that we have learned to endure between breaks in our favorite TV shows (okay, not if you have a DVR), articles in our favorite magazines, and pop-ups on our favorite web sites.

And as hard as marketers try to inject emotion and depth into their ads, they're still just ads. It's really hard to get someone to care deeply about a 30-second spot. Because the vehicle is empty.

MOVEMENTS ARE ROOTED IN PASSION

By their very definition, movements are born out of passion. Passion to unite and passion for change. There's nothing dry and emotionally detached about something in which you believe deeply. Because when you believe in something, you give yourself over to it. The desire to be a part of something bigger than yourself is hardwired into just about everyone's DNA. Think about the groups that people readily join and support: Religion. Sports teams. Even brands.

A former colleague at Brains on Fire was a huge Clemson University football fan. We should preface this by saying that not only did he not play for the football team at any time; he didn't even attend college at Clemson. But during football season—without fail—he'd come into work on Monday and say things like "Man, we really sucked this weekend" or "Did you see the game? We were awesome!" Do you notice that one word he uses? For you English geeks, it's the first-person plural pronoun: "we." Not "they" or "those guys" or "the Clemson football team." It's "we." As in "us." As in "we're in this thing together."

The dedicated football fan believes in—and therefore experiences the joys and pains of—something bigger than himself. That's passion. That's a willingness to sacrifice time and money and attention. That's the belief that Clemson's success is his success, and his success is Clemson's.

Movements sustain and grow this passion. A campaign can get people excited, but that burst of energy is hard to sustain. As Rob Morris from Love146 puts it, "A movement is not a spasm of passion." Because a movement moves—far beyond the initial hype.

CAMPAIGNS RELY ON TRADITIONAL MEDIA

Remember the good old days when marketers could influence and reach just about everybody with television, print, radio, and outdoor boards? Yes, we have that new-fangled Internet with the sponsored blogs and banners and pop-ups and paid-search results, but it's really just a modernization of the old ways. It's a 2.0 version of pushing out the messages of the command-and-control culture.

Advertising isn't going away, and we're certainly not attempting to bad-mouth a $500 billion industry. But we need to be very, very clear about the purpose of advertising: it's for *awareness*. If you have a new company, a new product, or a new service, you want people to know it exists. You want to make them *aware*.

So if you have the cash, you buy that Super Bowl spot and expose millions of eyeballs to your new baby. You make them aware (though you can't make them care) that you exist. The problem is that there's no credibility there. According to a 2009 Yankelovich Study, we live in a world where 76 percent of people believe that companies lie in ads, and people's trust that businesses will do the right thing has dropped from 58 percent in 2008 to a dismal 38 percent in 2009 (2009 Edelman Trust Barometer). We're betting that those figures don't take most marketers to their happy place.

But really, why *would* your audience believe that you are the best, or the most cost-effective, or have the greatest inventory? They don't know you. They probably don't have any experience with you. You're just another talking head in a sea of talking heads. It's like a stranger coming up to you at a bar and proclaiming that they are really smart, they get a lot of dates, and they make a lot of money. You have no idea if they are telling the truth. Sure, they are trying to make you aware that they believe those things about themselves, but if you don't know them, why should you trust them?

The conversation is lacking *credibility*.

MOVEMENTS RELY ON WORD OF MOUTH, WHERE THE PEOPLE ARE THE MEDIUM

Like it or not, your life is a marketing medium. Sure, it's the clothes you wear. The music you listen to. The car you drive. Your belief system. Even the words that come out of your mouth. But you yourself are a vessel. A vehicle that carries your hopes, thoughts, dreams, and especially your experiences.

This is where word of mouth comes into play. Now let's make one thing clear from the start: word of mouth has been around forever. The first caveman probably told the second caveman where the best hunting grounds were. However, the marketing world has really seen a heightened emergence of this trend in the past five years or so. That is, they've been trying to figure out how to harness that very powerful thing that happens when someone you know and trust makes a recommendation to you.

And while the purpose of advertising is driving awareness, word of mouth is where credibility comes into play. When you trust someone, you label them as "credible" in your world. So when they tell you something—especially something with which they have a personal experience—you believe them. It influences your purchasing decisions, your own opinions—and your life.

Is credibility better than awareness? It depends on the person you ask. But they both serve a very important role. The trick is figuring out the balance. How do they work hand in hand? What's the right mix in a world where awareness is a commodity, and trust is a rarity?

CAMPAIGNS ARE PART OF THE CREATIONIST THEORY

Not too long ago, a kindred spirit, John Moore from the Brand Autopsy Marketing Practice, wrote and spoke about the idea of which came first: marketing worthy of word of mouth, or word of mouth marketing. It's got great nuggets of the whole creation-versus-natural-evolution argument in it. But to take that idea a step further for the selfish purposes of comparing campaigns and movements: Campaigns are part of the creationist theory. In other words, "Let's create something cool so people will talk about it."

This idea is often applied to the company, product, or service side of things in that—and we just love hearing this—they are desperately trying to create the next big thing (as in the next Google, iPod, TiVo, etc.) because if they do, then everyone will talk about them, right? It's true. People will talk about your supercool product. But what are the chances of that product being created and reaching the success of Apple's iPod?

The other one we hear quite often is the "killer" theory. It seems there are legions of companies out there that are trying to kill and replace the market leaders. But all they seem to do is look like copycats. Face it: You're late to the game. And if you spend all your R&D, time, and energy obsessing over the market leader, you're screwed before you even come to market—because you're focused on what you're not, instead of on what you are. And you can't build a product—or an identity—on what you lack. So stop trying to "kill" anything, and instead, nurture and grow your own idea into something the likes of which has never before been seen. Soon enough, you'll be the one that everyone else is trying to kill.

And people don't just think that creating the next big product will get others to talk about them. They also think that if they create the next noteworthy, entertaining, amazing ad campaign, then people will talk about it. Enter the march of the Super Bowl hoopla.

A 30-second TV spot during the 2009 Super Bowl set advertisers back a cool $3 million, according to CBS News. The big ad shops tend to get more excited about making a name for themselves than about making money for their clients, so the ads have become the show within the show for the Super Bowl. And then we all sit around the next day discussing, ranking, and tearing them apart. For one day. Then the world moves on, and we quickly forget just about all of what we've seen. And we certainly can't seem to remember what most of the ads were for.

But a lot of marketers think, "If I could just create the next great ad campaign, then everything will be great." And good luck with that. It's the creationist theory hard at work.

MOVEMENTS ARE PART OF THE EVOLUTIONIST THEORY

Movements move. Actually, let us rephrase that: Movements move organically. Because, again, movements are made up of people. And when you hand the keys to the people who are truly passionate about that movement—you know the ones: the loud and proud, the evangelists, the quiet leaders—then I guarantee you that you'll ignite a movement.

Let's make sure to say this, though: No movement that we've ever helped ignite has gone according to plan. We learn along the way. But always, always, *always,* when we let people take the lead, they exceeded our expectations and ended up taking the movement to places that we never even could have imagined (and we have pretty big imaginations around here). Your employees and customers are *so* much closer to that product or service than you are. Sure, you know the book stuff: the demos, the numbers, the competition, the best time to put something on sale, or change out the lines. But very few marketers actually *live* it—and we're not talking about doing your job and working 80-hour weeks. We mean living and breathing and participating in your customers' lives.

So why not ask them to lead the way, to be the ones who help you succeed? Why not let them show you when and where and why your company needs to evolve?

CAMPAIGNS ARE YOU TALKING ABOUT YOURSELF

Don't throw a party and just expect people to show up. There are thousands of marketing "parties" out there, and more being thrown every day, especially online. Companies are screaming at the public: "*Hey! You there!* Come over here to my party. And while you're at it, talk about me. Aren't I great? I'm the best, right? Man, I'm so awesome! Wow. It ain't easy being this fantastic, but I try. I try."

Would you stick around at a party with that guy for very long? We wouldn't either. We all know that advertising adopts the push mentality; it's pushing messages on all of us in an aggressive form of one-way communication. Throwing a party and expecting people to show up is the push mentality disguised in sheep's clothing.

MOVEMENTS ARE OTHERS TALKING ABOUT YOU

Your company isn't what *you* say it is or want it to be; it's the stories that people tell about it. It's what your customers' friends, families, and neighbors say about you, based on what they heard from their friends, families, and neighbors.

Movements recruit by word of mouth, when like-minded people working together for a common cause look for other like-minded people. Think about this as you go about your day; how many times does a trusted friend or associate recommend a product, service, or idea to you? And more importantly, how many times do you act on those recommendations versus the number of times you take action on a media message? It's a no-brainer: Either you're talking about yourself and getting lost in the sea of messages, or your customers are talking about you.

" To put something out there where people can, and will comment, completely free, and we don't control it, is definitely a scary thing for us."

Tonya Polydoroff – Public Relations Specialist
for a large international company

CAMPAIGNS ARE AN ON-OFF SWITCH

Campaigns have a beginning and an end. There are periods when we throw the light switch on, create the latest campaign, change that tag line like we just love to do, and buy those media placements. Then, when the well is dry, we turn the light switch off, wait for the next round of money to be found in the upcoming quarter's budget, and do it all over again. And again. And again. On. Off. On. Off. On. Off. It's been going on for half a century, and it's really hard for a lot of marketers out there to question something that has created a multibillion dollar industry—and, you know, stuffs money in their pockets as well.

MOVEMENTS ARE A VOLUME DIAL

Stay with us here. Let's set the stage: There is no zero on the movement volume dial. Sometimes the people in the movement are really loud, and sometimes there's just a soft, constant buzz happening, but it never turns off, dies out, or fades away into nothingness.

And the great thing about the movement volume dial (stay with me, all you *This is Spinal Tap* fans) is that this dial goes to 11. And that's what you want for your movement—the people who are "one louder." Sure, the 10s are great. They actively promote your company. They are loyal. They are even evangelists. But the 11s are the ones some might consider the crazies. You know them: You think they love your company just a little too much; maybe they're a little too obsessed with that product. They can't help telling everyone they know how much they love your service.

We're here to tell you that you should embrace the 11s. Throw your arms wide open and love them. Open up and show them what your company is all about—the good and the bad. We all have a tendency to keep the 11s at arm's length. But why would you want to do that? Yes, they might need a little more attention, and they may be a tad high maintenance. But they sacrifice their time and money for you, and that's better than any ad campaign you could ever create.

CAMPAIGNS EMBRACE AN US-VERSUS-THEM MENTALITY

The mind-set under which we've all operated for decades goes hand in hand with the aforementioned war vocabulary. As marketers, we are always trying to get people to do things: Pay attention to our messages. Buy our products and services. We even try to get them to join our community or talk about us. It's us, the marketing department, against them, the customer.

Former director of communications for Fiskars Brands and longtime Brains on Fire client Suzanne Fanning recently sent us a piece of brilliance. When we asked her about how companies should "use" their customer ambassadors, she replied that companies shouldn't be looking to "use" anybody. All the rules of friendship, Fanning said, should apply to your relationship with your biggest fans. You don't try to get your friends to do things for you. You might ask them to help you, but it's definitely not a one-sided relationship. Friends don't expect anything from one another. You don't talk badly about them behind their backs. Friends are honest with one another. Friends value one another for who they are and what they stand for—it's the reason they're friends in the first place.

So when we start thinking of our biggest fans as our friends, we're able to step back and look at them completely differently. And fandom isn't a one-way street. Just because you have fans doesn't mean you shouldn't be fans of theirs. Love, after all, is a circular transaction, and the cool thing about it is that love always makes its way back to those who give it. It works in relationships, and it works in business. Wait a minute. Strike that. It works in relationships. Period. Business would not be business without relationships. So the quickest path to growth is to shower the people—the customers—you love with love. It's really the only way to meaningful growth and success. You love them. They love you. They spread the love. The love comes back. And the whole thing just keeps going and going.

MOVEMENTS SAY, "WE'RE ALL IN THIS TOGETHER"

There is no us versus them. There is just us. When you stand shoulder to shoulder with your customers and they stand shoulder to shoulder with you, the struggle ends. The war is over, and everyone wins. We're all in this together. Your customer's success is your success, and your success is your customer's. When you realize that, you start to think about how you can best work together instead of figuring out the most effective way to work against one another. You're reframing the conversation in the most fundamental way.

SO WHO INSIDE YOUR COMPANY SHOULD OWN THE MOVEMENT?

There's a constant debate going on inside companies about who should own the word-of-mouth practices, both inside and outside corporate walls. Is the marketing or public relations department more suited for it? What department should the ambassador program fit in? Who should be the champion for the customers?

And the debate rages on.

The answer is simple: whoever cares the most. It could be someone in the research department for all we care. But for a movement to work inside an organization, you have to have at least one person who has the courage it takes to get things done. To push decisions through. To fight when the time is right and explain when it's needed. To champion the cause and lead the way through the bureaucratic red tape. All it takes is one believer. One champion. Just one.

Even if you think it belongs in the marketing department, someone in the marketing department has to be a believer.

Angela Daniels is a lead ambassador for the Fiskateers, a movement ignited for and by Fiskars Brands, the company that makes the iconic orange-handled scissors: "My father-in-law owns a business. I talked to him about what the Fiskateers do. He hears the words but I think it's very hard for a traditional company to give up control. There is something that makes it so difficult for people to allow their fans to be fans."

ONE LAST THING

So now that we've gotten some of the blocking and tackling out of the way—now that we're all on the same page, and you've got the information you need—let's charge forward into an explanation of how you can actually ignite a movement.

One last thing: Take off your marketing hat. Seriously. It's ruining you. Well, at least sometimes it is. Because when we bring marketing into a relationship, we damage it. Nobody *wants* to be "marketed to." A great way to look at this is through the eyes of Justine Foo, a PhD of Neuroscience who contributes to the insight development of the movements at Brains on Fire: "The role of traditional branding is to influence behavior. The difference with movements is to inspire behavior." So don't try to influence; get out of that business. Now is the time to inspire. People don't want to be influenced. There's a negative connotation associated with that, like you're trying to control their minds and actions. But people long to be inspired. And inspiring them to action is a win-win.

> "The role of traditional branding is to influence behavior. The difference with movements is to inspire behavior."
>
> Justine Foo – PhD of Complex Systems and the Brain Sciences

So it's really, *really* important to remember to take off our marketing hats and just be people thinking about how to relate to other people in an honest, open, transparent way. Would you show up at some random person's house and scream from the doorstep that they should buy your stuff? Not likely.

Watching the Twitter stream on a daily basis, we see link after link after link teaching us how to be better marketers: "Twitter dos and don'ts," "How companies can use Facebook," "Why your company should be using social media." And while there are some great points (among all the junk), we are forgetting how to act as people. We, as marketers, are hypermarketing to other marketers. And it's too much.

So take the marketing hat off. And guess what? You don't even have to put a people hat on—because you are one. A person. An individual. A customer. A fan. A human who has all kinds of relationships. And when you start thinking like that, all the marketing mumbo jumbo will kick in and support it. But lead with the humanness. Lead with unmarketing. Because that will far outweigh and outlast the latest Twitter marketing topic. Every. Single. Time.

BRAINS
ON
FIRE

Lesson #1

Movements Aren't about the Product
Conversation; They're about the
Passion Conversation

Dear marketers: You've been brainwashed.

It's not your fault. It's the industry's fault. The four Ps. The unique selling proposition. The out-of-the-box approaches. Jeez. We've been preprogrammed to follow the processes that everyone else follows (even though we all call it something different), crank out the same work, enter the same award shows—and then complain about how our clients don't let us do any good work.

But the biggest thing we've been brainwashed to do is talk. A lot. About ourselves, our company, and our product. We talk about benefits. Enhancements. Upgrades—God, the upgrades. How much we care about you, and how our customer satisfaction is the highest around. Talk. Talk. Talk. Blah. Blah. Blah. Me. Me. Me. And then we get turned down and go back to the drawing board to try a different approach.

It's *hard* not to talk about yourself first, or try to make it all about your product and service. After all, that's what you get paid to do. However, talking about yourself won't make others talk about you. As *Tribal Knowledge* author John Moore puts it, "Buzz does not create evangelists; evangelists create buzz."

So you have to ask yourself, is it really all about you? Or is it about others?

"Buzz does not create evangelists; evangelists create buzz."

John Moore – Brand Autopsy

THE NEW PERSPECTIVE

There once was a local charity golf tournament where a putting contest was held at the end of the day. A dozen golfers signed up and paid to participate to claim the grand prize: two roundtrip tickets to anywhere in the continental United States. To win, you simply had to sink a 50-foot putt. The participating golfers lined up around a huge, undulating green. While one participant tried to make the putt, the others had to turn their backs so they could not "read the green."

Now, while a lot of people are far from being skilled golfers, one item of fairly common knowledge among golfers is that when it comes to putting, the green can play tricks on you. You can look at the putt from one angle and think the ball will do one thing and then get a completely different read from another angle. Any savvy golfer knows—at the very least—to always look at the cup from behind the ball and then look at the ball from behind the cup. As an instructor once said, "You want to see where the hole will welcome the ball."

The competitors were all decent golfers. Yet it was amazing to see how, as each walked up to the ball, he took a moment to look at the green and then just lined up and hit the ball. Not one of them ever even came close to making the putt. Not a single one of these guys—who knew better—ever walked around the green or stood behind the hole to get a better read. It was as if the moment there was prize money involved or people were watching, all of the fundamentals were forgotten. Maybe out of the corner of their eye, they could see what the person did before them and just assumed that was the way to do it.

How often do we see this phenomenon occur in business? We are all aware of how critical it is to look at what we do from both our customers' and our employees' perspective. Yet how often do we skip that step and instead rush to make the putt? How often do our eyes and minds play tricks on us? Sure, sometimes we're good enough to get it close, but in today's hypercompetitive market, is close really good enough?

REFRAME THE CONVERSATION

We've already determined that to start a movement, you have to come to terms with the fact that it's not about you. It never has been, and it never will be. So when you spend your advertising dollars talking about yourself, you are having a one-way conversation that you control (or at least have the illusion of control).

Something that is vital to success in developing both identities and movements is the need to reframe the conversation. Since we can't build a movement around the company, product, or service, we have to find the passion conversation and ignite the movement around whatever that may be. When we reframe the conversation, we allow people to look at it in a completely different way.

"Your company is the stories people tell about it."

Greg Cordell – Brains on Fire,
Chief Inspiration Officer

EXAMPLES? HERE ARE SOME FROM OUR OWN EXPERIENCE

Rage against the Haze

Ignited in 2002, Rage against the Haze is South Carolina's youth-led anti-tobacco movement.

In the late 1990s, The Master Tobacco Settlement was an agreement between the large tobacco companies and the Attorneys General of 46 states. In addition to agreeing to abandon certain marketing practices, particularly marketing to youth, settlement money was allocated to each state for tobacco prevention efforts. The nutshell is that the monies from the Tobacco Settlement spent in South Carolina were some of the lowest in the nation.

South Carolina also has the lowest tax on cigarettes, and some of the highest smoking rates. So some of state's younger citizens led a sustainable anti-tobacco movement that didn't use traditional media. They merely spread the word through peer-to-peer engagement.

But instead of focusing the conversation on fear and hatred of Big Tobacco, we chose to reframe the conversation. It wasn't about teens telling other teens not to smoke. It became a conversation about empowerment. We met teens where they were and just gave them the tools and platform they needed to express their opinions—about whatever their passion was: drug prevention, environmental responsibility, teen pregnancy, dropout rates, homelessness.

And as you'll read in these pages, reframing the conversation comes down to getting personal. Quentin James, one of the first teen leaders for the movement, said it wasn't about telling his friends not to smoke:

"For me, the moment that sparked everything was reading [a quote] from one of the tobacco industry executives who was asked if he would ever use one of his products and he said, 'No, I don't smoke that shit, I reserve that right for the dumb, the poor, the black, and the young.' And I don't exactly know why, but at that moment—I remember it—my passion was sparked. And I remember thinking to myself that I have the opportunity to find my voice in this movement."

Quentin didn't know anything about tobacco prevention. We met him at a youth government workshop that was teaching people how to debate and present court cases. He attended one of our sessions, he asked questions, and we wrote his name down because he was engaged. Quentin decided to take that step forward to find his voice. Involvement isn't something we can force on people. No one can make anyone else take that step. It's the difference between buying a product and *being* the product. And the Quentins of the world are the ones who make the difference.

The Fiskateers

If you've ever owned a pair of orange-handled scissors, then you know what Fiskars is. A 360-year-old company based in Finland, Fiskars has many different divisions—office, school, gardening— but the one we'd like to talk about is their crafting division, in particular, scrapbooking.

The company realized that they were stuck in commodity land with their crafting customers. On top of that, their brand research found that they were seen as the milk and saltine crackers of their industry. They were lacking in both passion and loyalty. After all, scissors and paper aren't that exciting, right? Do you think that people really gather together to talk about how much they love their scissors? The angle of the blade, and the lovely color of orange, and on and on and on? Yeah, right.

The first time we visited the Fiskars North American headquarters in Madison, Wisconsin, a product engineer told us that he didn't know why anyone would really care about scissors. "I don't know why anyone would share their life with us, or share what they do about us." The employees simply did not see a connection between what they make and what people create.

But how do you reframe a conversation about paper and scissors? By listening to the words that come out of crafters' mouths. So with some digging, we soon found that it's not about the paper and scissors. It's about what people *do* with the paper and scissors: create amazing works of art that capture memories and are given away or passed down from generation to generation.

Fiskars becomes the conduit to their passion. The enabler. And therefore, Fiskars and its products become a natural part of the conversation.

IndieBound

The American Booksellers Association (ABA) is the national trade association for independent booksellers and offers support and guidance on a number of key issues. One of the biggest challenges small stores face is how to compete with the huge volume of marketing and awareness the big-box retailers can generate. For seven years, ABA had been running a marketing program of sorts called BookSense for their members. But BookSense was dated, and most independents were not participating or even seeing value in the program.

The ABA needed more than a program; they needed a movement. A rallying cry. A way to give independent booksellers a voice. And that voice was found in IndieBound.

Do you think it's easy for your local neighborhood bookstore to compete with the Amazons and Barnes & Nobles of the world these days? Not quite. So the conversation can't just be about selling books; it has to focus on some kind of distinction between the places where people can buy them. Reframing the conversation for this group meant celebrating the independent, entrepreneurial spirit that made them want to start their own bookstores in the first place. It's about shopping local and building community—not just for independent booksellers, but for all independent stores.

Chief Marketing Officer for the American Booksellers Association Meg Smith puts it in her own words: "We were able to identify what the missing emotion was. It was this sense of belonging, community and real attraction to independence, and that had evolved over the years," she said.

This was the idea behind IndieBound, a movement of independent booksellers that Meg calls a perfect combination of time and place and knowledge, the things we learned, the things that were brought to us, and the things that were happening out in the world. "People are able to identify themselves with an emotional concept—and maybe that's what the movement is. It's this emotional identification that we didn't really have the language for before," she says.

The Park Angels

There are more than 100 public parks in Charleston, South Carolina, a city that simply doesn't have the funds it needs to support all those spaces. So the Charleston Parks Conservancy (CPC) was created to help.

But when it came time for the CPC to define who they are and what they stand for, the group quickly realized that they couldn't be just another public service organization in this historic city. And they couldn't be about picking up trash or planting trees. So they reframed the conversation. Today, the Charleston Parks Conservancy is about connecting people to the past, people to people, and people to their parks. This allows them—and the people of Charleston—to look at their parks in a completely different light.

Mi11

Electronics retail giant Best Buy has recently started selling high-end musical instruments in about 100 store-within-store locations throughout the country. We're talking high-end guitars, drums, keyboards and mixing equipment.

Now, there are a lot of challenges that emerge for a big-box retailer that attempts to enter this category—like, for instance, how people don't want to buy a Fender Stratocaster and a kitchen stove from the same salesclerk. So how does a Fortune 75 company reframe the conversation when it comes to selling instruments that they don't even make themselves?

After talking with the people who work within the Musical Instrument (MI) space at Best Buy, we found out that it's not about selling instruments. It's about the everyday life-changing moments that happen when they put a guitar in the hands of a kid for the first time, or meet that 65-year-old who's falling back in love with music again. So it's not about selling; it's about unlocking. Unlocking and celebrating the music we all have inside. And from that, Mi11 was born.

However, talking about the actual products can, in fact, enter into the mix. Jamie Plesser from Best Buy's Marketing Strategy and Communications explains, "Part of the passion conversation is actually the product itself. People who are really passionate about playing or making music are inherently passionate about the gear."

"Part of the passion conversation is actually the product itself. People who are really passionate about playing or making music are inherently passionate about the gear."

Jamie Plesser – Best Buy
Consumer Marketing Manager

IT'S REFRAMING THE CONVERSATION

It's turning the funnel on its head, giving up on the "me" mentality, and making it about "us." We're in this together. People want to be a part of something bigger than themselves because everyone wants to be bigger than they are. So when you have a conversation about how *you* can fit into *their* lives—instead of the other way around—you reframe the conversation and give them a chance to own it.

Justine Foo, a kindred spirit, sums it up nicely: "Reframing the conversation is about going from what role does our product play in people's lives, to what role can we play? It's from a product role to a social role."

"Reframing the conversation is about going from what role does our product play in people's lives to what role can we play? It's from a product role to a social role."

Justine Foo – PhD of Complex Systems
and the Brain Sciences

SIMPLE? NEVER. EFFECTIVE? ABSOLUTELY

You might have noticed in each of these cases that we're not looking for shared passion when we look for people to be involved in a movement. We're just looking for passion. Period. When you bring people together, then the shared passion emerges. People unite based on the enthusiasm that brought them to the table—which they can now share with one another. The anti-tobacco message is the expression of one group's passion. Crafting is an expression of the Fiskateers' passion. What makes the community great is the different flavors of passion, and how everyone involved wants to share it.

WHY AM I LOOKING FOR THE PASSION CONVERSATION AGAIN?

Because people connect through shared interests, and passion is the key to a sustainable movement, not to mention the best competitive advantage. It's the things we're most passionate about that we want to talk about. Sir Ken Robinson, PhD, sums it up this feeling up well in his book *The Element*. "Connecting people who share the same passions affirms that you are not alone. Finding your tribe brings the luxury of talking shop, of bouncing ideas around, of sharing and comparing techniques . . ."

It's the remarkable experiences that inspire us that we want to share with other people. And it's passion that separates a sustainable movement from a short-term campaign.

Building movements requires us to understand not only what people are saying about your products and services but also how your offerings allow customers to do what they love, or do it better. This is the passion conversation.

So find the passion you share with your customers, and support it. It gives your customers a reason to love you that the competition cannot easily supersede, because it's not about a product feature that can be replicated.

And while you're looking for that passion, remember this: Passion can be a scary thing, because it can't be imitated, feigned, or bottled up. So treat it with the care and respect that it deserves, because passion isn't a commodity.

PASSION STARTS WITH PURPOSE

There's an old (unverified) story of an unannounced visit that President John F. Kennedy made to the space center at Cape Canaveral sometime in the 1960s. Kennedy toured the complex and met a man in janitor's clothing. "What is it you do here?" he asked. The man replied, "Earn a living." Kennedy nodded and moved on. He met another man in janitor's clothing and asked him the same question. "I pick up all the trash," the man said. Kennedy grinned and walked on until he met yet another man in the same outfit and asked the question once again. This time a big smile grew across the man's face as he replied, "Mr. President, I'm helping to put a man on the moon."

You can't have passion without purpose. The two are intertwined. What are you passionate about? And why are you passionate about it? Now, how does that connect you with a sense of purpose? That part of you that believes you're making a difference or standing up for something you believe in?

THE PASSION CONVERSATION NEEDS TO BE INTERNAL AND EXTERNAL

If you're doing some things right—and your company has made it through the Great Recession of 2009—then you just might have some fans out there. Fans have passion; it comes with the territory. And while it's a great thing to have, allow us to ask you this: Is it a lopsided kind of love? In other words, do your customers love your company or product or service more than you and your employees do?

Because if they do, you might be in trouble. Passion needs to be a mirror—something that's equal inside and outside a company. And if it's lopsided, you need to find out why.

If there's passion inside the company—from the very top to the good folks on the front lines—then you're easily going to find passion outside your company. But if your people are coming to work just to collect a paycheck, then you're not finding much passion inside or outside your walls.

Passion is contagious. It's exciting. It fuels word of mouth. And we've talked about how it's no longer a product conversation—it's no longer about you and what you can do. It's about finding out how you fit into people's lives and how you can be a conduit to their passion. You're the enabler, not the destination.

So follow the passion. It'll let you know very soon what's working and what's not. A great way to do so is to ask questions internally that will push your leadership and employees out of what they've come to know as their "job." We're looking to find out if a company believes that it truly matters. And here are some thought-starting questions to do just that.

If We Randomly Chose One of Your Employees and One of Your Customers and Put Them in a Room Together, Would a Passionate Brand Lovefest Break Out between These Two Strangers?

Seriously. Take old Jimmy down in purchasing and a random every-once-in-a-while customer. Lock the door, pass the popcorn, and see what happens. Where is the common ground? Sure, they can talk about great services and products, but when the lovefest breaks out, they'll be knee-deep in stories that revolve around your culture. They are both part of a community. The lines between employee and customer fade away, and all that's left are two fans. Kindred spirits. People who love what you stand for.

If Your Company Were (Heaven Forbid) to Be Hit by a Bus Tomorrow and Exterminated, Would Your Brand Live On without You? In Other Words, Is Your Customer's Brand Loyalty So Strong That It's Self-Sustaining?

Are you the main driver of what your brand stands for? Is it in the ads that the marketing department prints in the monthly pubs? Or does it live in the hearts and minds of your employees and customers? Brands that truly matter can, without a doubt, answer this question in a heartbeat. The culture of fans is so loyal that the brand they love so much will live on, even if it's not there to feed them anymore. And if something happened to you and your company, there would be an outcry from your fans. They wouldn't be happy about it at all. Calls would be made. E-mails would circulate. You would be mourned. But, in your absence, those who love you would pull together and somehow continue the word you'd begun.

Can Your Brand Cross Its Heart and Make an Ironclad Promise to Your Customers? Do You Know What That Promise Is?

The kinds of individuals you want attracted to your brand can easily find its core: the promise. The masses that blindly follow any big, glitzy ad campaign (insert your least favorite megaconsumer megacorporation here) will one day come to realize that's all it is—glitz, and no substance.

It's extremely scary to make a promise to your customers (and employees)—your fans—and genuinely mean it. Few can really do it. Now nowhere in this conversation do I want to lose sight of the fact that we're all in business to have fun, make money, and change the world; it's not all about feelings and lovefests. But it has to start with something: a promise. And if you can clearly tell people, in a couple of sentences, what that promise is, then you're already ahead of the pack. And if you can also deliver on it—well, then you've really got something.

Do You Have Talented People Invading You with Resumes? Are the Best of the Best Dying to Work for You?

Everybody wants to stand for something and, ideally, find a job they love, but very few of us actually manage to combine those two elements. So, are the resumes and cover letters you get the standard slew of endless "Key Objectives" and "Relevant Experience" that have been sent out to 45 other companies? Or are people doing anything and everything they can to get an interview with you? Is their contact with you overflowing with passion? If you're doing it right, you never have to post a job opening. There's always a wealth of talent just waiting to work for their favorite brand.

If You Threw an Optional Employee Party, How Many of Your Employees Would Attend?

Do you have an internal culture of kindred spirits? Sure, just like any family that spends 40-plus hours a week together, there will be the occasional spat and disagreement. But it's still a family, people who care about each other, with a common cause that binds them together. And they live and breathe your brand. But more important, they don't merely have a job. They have made a choice to be a part of something they believe in. It isn't about earning a paycheck; it's about being an extension of a product or service.

Is the Entrepreneurial Inspiration That Gave Birth to Your Company Still Alive and Well? Prove It

Unfortunately, most people's idea of fulfilling the American dream is largely based on chasing that almighty dollar. But most companies were originally founded on something much bigger than that. A nugget of inspiration can take an industry from tired to inspired. The proverbial better mousetrap. So is whatever it was that brought about your company still easily recognizable—and can you say in one brief sentence that is it still true?

Remember the story from earlier in the chapter about the janitor who worked at NASA? When asked what he did for a living, he replied, "I'm helping to put a man on the moon." Does everyone in your company from the CEO down to the mailroom know what you're working toward? And is it more than being the biggest and making the most money?

Does the World Know about Your Brand Solely through Traditional Media Advertising and Promotion? Or Do You Rely on That Effective and Efficient Word-of-Mouth Advertising?

Pop quiz: If tomorrow Congress passes a law that makes TV, radio, billboards, and print ads illegal, would your company survive? In a strange sort of way, this is already happening. It's not a law, of course; it's consumers bulletproofing themselves to those traditional methods of reaching them. (Not to mention technologies like TiVo that allow people edit out commercials altogether.)

If what you make, do, or offer truly matters, then you have fans who are spreading the word about your products, services, and culture like a virus (a good one) to their coworkers, friends, family, and strangers they meet in the grocery store line. It's like they've discovered a secret that's so good, they can't keep it to themselves.

Are Your Employees Encouraged and Empowered to Speak Their Minds—or Shut Up and Work?

Do you see a theme developing here? Deep beliefs breed passion, and when passion oozes throughout a culture, you're going to attract people who will speak up on its behalf. Just start a conversation about religion or politics, and watch this theory in action. And duck while you're at it!

So, have you beaten your employees into submission? Are you suffering from "not invented here" syndrome? Are the only good ideas your ideas? For companies that truly matter, an open-door policy is really an open soapbox. We're not talking about screaming matches, just discussions where people use the term "fall on a sword." Your employees are your greatest assets; any good CEO realizes that. Your next big idea could be outside your door in cubicle land.

Do Your Financial Goals Have a Death Grip on Your Trachea?

There's no denying that the bottom line is important, and nobody ever complained about making a lot of money. But if that, and that alone, is the driving force behind your company, then maybe it's time to revisit "Is the Entrepreneurial Inspiration That Gave Birth to Your Company Still Alive and Well?"

What Is So Important about Your Brand That You Would Work on It without Compensation?

If you know what it is, then write it down on a piece of paper and frame it, because it's your new credo. Are you the head of a company or the head of a cause? Or both? Are you satisfied at the end of the day with what you've accomplished for the bigger picture? Very few companies out there exist for no reason. Even those who have lost sight of what they stand for can still find—buried under corporate politics and corner offices—a glimmer of the inspiration that first started it all. And sometimes they just have to go back and dig it out of the rough again.

Let's be honest. There's nothing really groundbreaking here; it's just common sense. And it's the same stuff that all great brands have been built on for ages. Emotion. Inspiration. A culture of fans. Brands that truly matter have an edge over their competition. If you can give positive answers to all of the preceding questions, then you're on the right track (and now you just have to learn how to stay there). If you couldn't answer the questions, then you might have some soul-searching to do.

Customers are like adolescents with attention deficit disorder in a room full of shiny objects. They might take a look at you initially, but you're never going to hold their attention unless they believe and soon become a fan. Blessed be the CEO who figures this out first and lets it permeate every aspect of the company. Not only will the company be profitable but also it will be able to build a culture that would leave a hole in the world if it disappeared. And that's a sure sign that it truly matters.

HOW DO YOU FIND THE PASSION CONVERSATION?

Okay, gather around, lean in real close, and we'll tell you how to find the passion conversation for your company, product, or service. Ready?

You participate.

To figure out what people's passion is, you have to talk to them. Spend time with them. Participate in their lives.

Quality insight is more important that quantity. Taking the time to really understand people is more important than having a strategy by next week. Traditional market research has its role; after all, if you don't know who your customers are, then you don't know who you should be talking to.

But you can't truly know people through paper or surveys, because some things just don't translate. You have to sit down with them. Listen to their reality, to their joys, to what keeps them up at night. You have to come to understand the world from their unique individual points of view, because the seeds of a movement lie somewhere in those conversations.

We can guess all day long about what motivates employees and customers. But if you stay up in your ivory tower and look down on all the people, more than likely, you're going to start to assume things. And we all know what happens when you make assumptions. There is a much higher quality of learning that comes from actual, real-life participation versus what you get with "agency insight" or "discovery." In other words, it's one thing to read the manual; it's something else to put the damn thing together.

Quite simply, participating in employees' and customers' lives allows you to walk a mile in their shoes. It allows you to crawl inside their heads and go beyond those superficial, surface-level answers that people give at parties when you ask them "What do you do for a living?" It's part curiosity and part anthropology. You have to want to know what drives them—beyond just doing a job. Being naturally curious has a lot to do with finding out the core motivations that live inside a person. And besides, it can be a lot of fun.

If you had to put it into a stuffy, agency-speak bucket, it would be called "qualitative insight." But go deeper than that. Ask unexpected questions. Push comfort zones. Don't just inquire about their jobs; ask both employees and customers about their lives. And then listen to the words that come out of their mouths. You want there to be a mirror—that the same passion felt internally is felt externally as well. And the passion that is felt externally can fuel that internal passion. There's a constant cycle of excitement.

Participation can open your eyes and bring you new experiences, too. Our crew has delivered dry cleaning in Boston, mowed lawns in Florida, ridden on moving trucks in Kansas City, and worked the floor at a big-box retail store in LA. We've been to all-night scrapbooking events in Chicago, hung out with engineers in Omaha, and run the rivers with kayakers in Tennessee. All to dig for what the passion conversation was.

IT DOESN'T END WITH PARTICIPATION

However, the terms "participation" and "engagement" are both being thrown around a lot these days. And they're also being interchanged—something we think is a big mistake, a mistake that is further clouding the word-of-mouth marketing waters.

There's a distinction between the two. Can you tell which word belongs to which definition? One is "to take or have a part or share, as with others; partake; share," and the other is "to occupy the attention or efforts of." In other words, *participation* does not equal *engagement*.

When you go to your meetings today, you'll see the difference between those who merely sit in the meeting and participate solely by showing up, and those who add to the conversation because they are engaged. You can participate without being engaged. Engagement is the step beyond participation.

"Participation ≠ Engagement."

Robbin Phillips – Brains on Fire,
Courageuos President

So many companies are just seeking participants (friends or followers) in their word-of-mouth and social media efforts. "Come participate in our campaign. Upload your videos and pictures. Come on, be present, so we can count you and your eyeballs for our metrics." But those who engage—those who earn "the attention or efforts of" (especially the efforts)—are the ones who are building something that will last. It's the beginning of a movement. Which would you rather have?

BUT I DON'T HAVE A SEXY PRODUCT LIKE GUITARS AND KAYAKS

Though you're certainly not alone, you'd be surprised to see what people can get excited about. Remember, Fiskars sells scissors. That's not very sexy to the average person. And to be honest, it's not all that sexy to the average crafter (who is their main audience). But remember: It's not about you talking about your product.

It's about people celebrating how your product fits into their lives and how you enable them to use it.

The maker of oil in a spray can, WD-40, has a fan club. Yes. Fans of oil in a spray can. Sharpie has legions of fans—and they make markers. Markers, people! Is it harder for you to find the passion conversation if you're the owner of, say, a carpet-cleaning chemical business or a mulch company? No, it's not. Because it's still getting in the right frame of mind and talking to your employees and customers, not about your product or service, but about their lives. And in those passion conversations will you find your place in their lives.

Movements Start with the
First Conversation

We're often asked, "So, when does the movement actually start?" A lot of people assume that it takes place when the web site is up, all the online and off-line tools are produced, the launch party happens, and the fanfare ensues.

Nope. Not even a little bit.

The advertising and marketing industry is addicted to the "reveal." We like to go off into a corner, think of all this cool stuff (whether it's relevant to solving our client's problems or not), and then come back with this huge "TA-DA!" moment. It's all part of the magic act. But you can't ignite a movement on the reveal. Movements don't start when you pull the trigger and execute tactics. You can't ignite them without people. People are, after all, the killer app.

But guess what we've learned about igniting movements? They start with that first one-on-one conversation, because, as Best Buy's Jamie Plesser says, "A conversation is an experience in and of itself." Yes, the *idea* is big, but it starts small, by huddling little groups of kindred spirits together and letting them own it. It's hard for individuals to feel like they own your latest ad campaign, no matter how touching, personal, and compelling it might be. You're not talking solely to me; you're talking to millions of other people and hoping they will upload a video at your site talking about you.

"A conversation is an experience in and of itself."

Jamie Plesser – Best Buy
Marketing Strategy and Communication

What you don't want to hear about is that small takes a little more time than big. It takes patience and a plan that sees further than six weeks into your strategy. Small is a lot deeper than big.

But small grows. Small nurtures the acorns instead of trying to rent the oaks. And small becomes bigger than big and goes the distance.

Small is not the new big. Small is the same small it always was. And if you start small, big gets bigger as you go along.

So yes, movements begin with the first conversation, that small group of deeply passionate and deeply dedicated people who believe. And plan. And pour blood, sweat, and tears into going out, finding kindred spirits, looking them in the eye, and talking with them about how they would shape this thing. They ask questions about engagement and participation, plant seeds, and ignite excitement. And the great thing about this laborious process is that it gets people talking with their friends in their own language about what they're helping to start.

We've already established that finding the passion conversation is the first step toward an authentic movement. But you have to actually talk to people to find that passion. And having conversations in a vacuum doesn't allow the natural contagion of conversation. People—both outsiders and insiders—want to talk. Asking for a conversation makes it easier to ask for involvement. It's an initial measure of what level of conversation a company's customers are having. It always establishes up front that a company is committed to having an open relationship and allowing—even encouraging—its customers to have authentic conversations.

But to ignite that movement with the first conversation, there are few things you need to keep in mind.

WE DON'T KNOW WHAT WE DON'T KNOW

It's okay. The world isn't going to crumble if you don't have the answer because you don't have all the answers. But the beautiful thing is that you can always go find them.

One of our mantras around the halls of Brains on Fire is "We don't know what we don't know." It keeps us honest and fuels our fire for listening. Because it's pretty frightening in today's expert-laden world that somebody can think they can tell a client exactly what they should be doing.

The hidden question behind "We don't know what we don't know" is "What are you going to do about it?" Instead of doing all the talking, let your customer and their customers do all the talking. It's a far more important job to sit back and listen and gain some insight on what you don't know.

Half of the entire movement-igniting process is based on having conversations with people. Now, be honest: Did your mind just go to online conversations? Blogs and message boards and exchanging tweets? But you are wrong. We go talk to people (wait for it . . .) face-to-face. Spend time in their presence. Walk a mile or seven in their shoes. Listen to the words that come out of their mouths. That's where the success of the movement takes root on so many levels. It's not about what *you* think. It's not about your philosophies or your gut or what your brochure is going to say. It's about what you don't know, the hidden nuggets that lie deep within the real, honest, transparent conversations you have. Not interviews. Not focus groups. Not surveys. Real words that come out of real people's mouths.

Success comes from admitting that you don't know what you don't know. And the sooner you humble yourself and realize that you're not an expert at everything your customers do, the better off you are. That's when you can begin to take off your marketing hat and wear no hats—just be a human being, one who is talking to other human beings and learning from them. That's where movement begins.

BURN THE NONDISCLOSURE AGREEMENT

Seriously. Take a match to it, and get rid of it. (Well, maybe after you resuscitate the lawyers from their heart attacks.)

Look, we understand the need for keeping secrets and not letting your competition know what you are doing. But you're paranoid, and that kind of thinking makes it easy to fall into that "us versus them" mentality, which really signals that you can't trust your employees and customers. Feeling that you have to protect yourself is a huge red flag, because when you hide behind the nondisclosure agreement, you're putting a gag order on a movement.

Believe it or not, you *want* people to talk about what you're doing. You *want* them to spread the word; after all, that's what word-of-mouth marketing is all about, and that's how movements get ignited. If you preface conversation with a customer by saying, "Okay, here's what we want to do. And by the way, don't tell anybody," or if you preface a conversation with a customer with a legal document, don't you think it's going to set a weird tone for the ensuing conversation? You're basically saying, "Hey there. How's it going, 'friend'? I don't trust you, but I want to pump you for information. How about you sign this document full of legal mumbo jumbo that says we'll take your firstborn if you mention anything to anyone, and then we'll get started?" It's not exactly the best way to start a meaningful relationship, is it?

Honesty. Transparency. Openness. These are words that are used a lot these days in the marketing world. And they point to the fact that the best relationships don't come with conditions or contracts.

If you have a conversation with your customer that is filled with honesty, transparency, true interest, and a *lot* of listening, then you've planted the first seed. The movement has begun in one mind and one heart. And that's usually the beginning of something powerful, meaningful, and full of potential that gets realized more every day.

A CASE FOR AGENCY VISIBILITY

In a lot of situations, agencies are asked to step back into the shadows and not be a visible part of implementation. But we'd like to make the case that agencies need to be visible part of the mix. It's part of being truly transparent, and it delivers other benefits as well.

When we ignite a movement, not only do the leaders (customers or employees) know that we are Brains on Fire and we are working with Best Buy or Fiskars or whomever; the entire community knows it as well. So we feel very much a part of the movement. It's not something that we crafted and then sent on its way. We are members. We know people in the community by name, and they know us by name, too. They know the role we play—solving information technology problems, managing the community in general, answering questions—whatever is needed.

The other benefit is that since everybody knows the roles of all the parties involved, we can be the heavy when we have to be. So the community around the brand can share their love all day long, and the brand itself is the good guy. Then when it comes time to take action, or discipline, or even say, "No," that's our job—and the brand is still golden.

REMEMBER, IT'S PASSION, NOT PRODUCT

When we were looking for leaders for the Fiskars movement, we put out a call to scrapbooking shops in Los Angeles, Sacramento,

Chicago, and Charlotte, and we told them what we were trying to accomplish. Did we know exactly what the movement would look like? Not at all. But we did know what our goals were. We didn't ask them to put the word out to the customers who spent the most money; we wanted to talk to their most passionate customers. The other important aspect is that we didn't want to talk to them about the product. Instead, we asked them to bring in their creations. Their work. Their art. And open it up and show us. *That's* where the passion comes in—how they love getting together with others and crafting. Or how they love to introduce crafting to others who don't think that they are creative. That's where you see the eyes light up and hear the stories. It's such a natural conversation. Because that's what they talk about on a daily basis.

Then we told them that we were interested in igniting a movement and looking for leaders. We admitted that we weren't crafters and that we needed their help. We told them that the success of the movement depended on them. We shared everything that we were thinking, not only to open the doors and show them everything to get their input but also to empower them.

Getting crafters in on the ground level created buy-in. It not only planted the seeds for the movement; it propelled the groundswell to begin. The people we talked to quickly started to spread the word to their friends and fellow crafters by informing them, "Keep an eye on Fiskars. They're doing something that I helped them with." We didn't ask them to do it, but we didn't tell them that they *couldn't* do it, either.

So they spread the word. They became empowered. They realized that this wasn't a marketing and PR stunt to try to get them to buy more stuff. This was real. This was theirs.

Soon after we chose our leads for the movement, Fiskateer #003 from Chicago, Illinois, wrote us:

> I believe that this will be an amazing success, [and that] the Fiskateers will bring [people] together to interact,

question, praise, discuss, involve, and change the world of crafting, and possibly some of the world at large, all in one program. We hope to host charity crops, raise money for worthy causes, involve you in your life and in your community in a tangible way, as well as help you to be the crafters you want to be. We hope to give you support, praise, and a place to call home in the crafting community. I feel so blessed to be a part of a program like this as we are just getting started. I think that we are on the verge of something great here, and I truly believe we are going to make a difference. So, here is where I become a dork. Not just a geek, or nerd, but true hard-core dork . . . and I am very aware of it! I did it to prove my point of being in this for the long haul and dedicated to this program. If it makes me the dorkiest of dorks, I don't care. . . .

And then she sent us a picture of her and her personalized license plate for her car that read: FISKTER 3.

This is from a crafter, in her own words, not coached by Fiskars or Brains on Fire. And it's what can happen when you empower the people who can make or break your company. These crafters have ownership in something bigger than themselves, and not many things are more powerful than ownership.

THE FIRST CONVERSATIONS ALLOW THE OPPORTUNITY FOR A STORY

When you're igniting a movement and openly ask for people to get involved on the ground level, you're helping them create a story. And stories can be very powerful.

Love146 founder Rob Morris (whom we met in the introduction) claims that stories are so important to customers because—unlike statistics—they can place themselves in the story: "There's no place for 'me' in [statistics]; I don't see myself there if it doesn't affect me. But I can actually see myself [in the context of story] and say 'Wow, I can play a part in this story by not being a bystander and involving myself in this. I can create something here and change the story by my involvement.' And that's the brilliance of story," Morris explains.

Stories are powerful, especially when they're personal. And while they can help build movements, let's be clear that these stories aren't your next TV ad. They aren't there to be exploited. And they certainly aren't your next slogan.

> Because stories live forever. Slogans live until the ad agency gets tired of them.
> Stories are real. Slogans are made up.
> Stories pull you in. Slogans try to push out a message.
> Stories are deep. Slogans are shallow.
> Stories are personal. Slogans are impersonal.
> Stories are passed on by word of mouth. Slogans are forced on us by ads.
> Stories are a part of who we are. After all, you don't tell slogans about your grandfather, or how your parents met, or even how you were treated at a restaurant.

Some folks feel the need to have slogans. And if it helps them sleep better at night, then that's great. But we'd rather hear a story and make our own decisions about what that company means to us, instead of a company (that we don't trust) trying to force their ideas of who they are on us.

Would you rather Love146 tell you that they are out to end child sex slavery in the world or hear a story of how they came to be? Would you rather hear a slogan for the Park Angels of the Charleston Parks Conservancy about caring for your cities' public spaces, or engage them in a conversation to talk about their own stories? Would you rather IndieBound cram a slogan about buying from your local bookseller down your throat, or hear their story told through a manifesto?

Slogans are a part of the ad world's history, and I'm not saying that they are the worst thing that's ever happened. I'm just agreeing with the Made to Stick guys:

> How do you know if you're inadvertently sloganeering? Here's a take-home test: If you can envision two exclamation points at the end of your idea, it's a slogan. If you can see it on a mug in Comic Sans font, it's a slogan. Toss it and start communicating.
>
> When you have a big idea, make it come alive with a story. Make it real, color in some details, let it be something people can care about. Just don't make it snappy.

SOUL IS A KEY INGREDIENT

So follow the bouncing ball. Movements start with the first conversation. Those conversations create stories. And those stories connect people. But it can be argued that ad campaigns also have stories. Ah, but ad campaigns are not sustainable because they have no soul. People bring soul into the picture. And soul just happens to breathe life into movements.

Soul can't be replaced by your technology platform, it can't be duped by your influential blogger outreach strategy, and it can't be duplicated by a hollow effort to build a community because that's really just another push mechanism with the illusion of engagement.

Soul is immaterial, full of emotion, and comes from people—not platforms. Soul begins deep within the recesses of your chest. It's wrapped in what you stand for, and it permeates every aspect of what you do and say.

So do you want to know why that shiny online community you built failed? Because you forgot something. You started with the tech and not the soul. And you're just another URL in a sea of meaningless portals that are begging people to come to their party and talk about their brand. That's soulless.

Is it easy to find soul? Not always. Sometimes it's as plain as the nose on your face, but you often have to dig. Talk to people face-to-face. Participate in their lives and not just their conversations. Only then can you even begin to understand what makes them tick and, if you're very lucky, get a glimpse of their soul.

THE FIRST CONVERSATIONS GET BUY-IN

When you sit down in front of people, look them in the eye, and have a genuine conversation with them, start by being honest about what you're trying to accomplish and quickly follow with "What do you think?" You're essentially asking for buy-in and admitting that you don't know everything. When you throw open the curtains and reveal your company's faults and needs to an outsider, they begin to become vested and get involved. You are no longer big company X sitting on the other side of the table; you are a human in a company made up of humans who are fallible. You are admitting that you need help. And that's pretty damn refreshing in today's day and age.

So your customers—especially those who have already shown interest—begin to realize that they can play a part in your success. They aren't a quota on a market research list that you have to check off before you can go home that day. There are no tricks up your sleeve. And if you really listen to them, then they know you're sincere, and you'd be surprised how they want to help.

And the great thing is that you just planted a seed of ownership. The people you've talked to will now take it upon themselves to ensure what they're a part of and what they've given input for is going to be a success. They have a story they can tell others, along with the recommendation to keep an eye on you—because you're doing something remarkable. And you better believe that they're going to spread the news. After all, the first to know is the first to tell. Not only will they tell others, they will do their part to make sure you're successful, because now their reputation depends on it.

The other aspect of this is collaboration. You're identifying people with whom you can have conversations, and approaching them in an authentic way. You're not using them for information and then leaving after you get what you need, because you need so much more than just information. You need them to be on your team, and the only way to make them feel that way is to avoid pumping them for information and actually collaborate with them.

So work on accomplishing the task at hand with one another. Remember, it's not "us versus them." It's "we're all in this together." When you do, the reward is buy-in—for both parties. Yes, it does go both ways, because you're beginning to invest in their lives as well. It's a two-way street that's paved with a solid foundation. You're cultivating relationships with people who will be your brand's friends and supporters in the future. These people are the folks who will stand up for you and also tell you like it is. Your advocates. Your evangelists. Your lifesavers.

WHO SHOULD YOU BE TALKING TO?

The hand-raisers. The people who have taken the time to write you love letters. The people who have referred business to you. Your biggest fans, or even just the biggest fans of your industry. Not the most influential, but the most passionate. What? You don't think you have any? Then look for them. Ask your employees. Go to your retail partners' stores and ask them to help. Yes, even go online and use simple, free monitoring tools to search blogs, message boards, and social media sites for your company or industry. You just might be surprised at what you find. It's an eye-opening experience, to say the least.

And when you find these kindred spirits, talk *with* them. Have a conversation, human to human. Come with some questions that can move the conversation along, but be open to the possibility of it zigging and zagging. Let it flow organically and, above all, let it be about them—not you or your product or service. It might take everything within you to fight that urge to tell your own stories, but fight it. Talk about them and their lives, and we guarantee that after they feel comfortable with you, they'll open up. A remarkable thing will happen next: Your brand will then naturally find its way into the conversation. Only then are you really planting the seeds of a movement and truly learning about the passion conversation, because it started with them—not you. It wasn't brand talking to consumer; it was person-to-person. When we all take off our masks, let down our guards, and dump the hidden agendas, then we can really listen to what the passion conversation is. And you better believe that it starts with that first conversation.

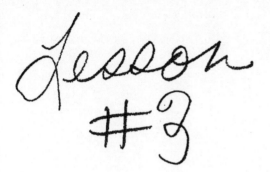

Movements Have Inspirational Leadership

Let's go ahead and get the whole talk about influence out of the way—a debate that's been raging on for a while now. On one side of the aisle, you've got Malcolm Gladwell and his tipping point theory, which boils down to how a select few folks are the ones who start the trends. They are the early adopters, the mavens, the influential ones. Also on this side of the aisle is Ed Keller's book *The Influentials,* whose premise claims that "one out of every ten Americans tells the other nine how to vote, where to eat, and what to buy." Keller's research shows that these people are "market multipliers"—people who are disproportionately asked for their advice by others and as a result are more likely to offer recommendations.

Based on these theories—which seem to make total sense when one initially considers them—the rage today is for agencies and brands to try to find these prized influencers, these people with huge blog audiences or tens of thousands of followers on Twitter. They think that if they can seed their product with that group, then not only will they tell their networks about it, but since they are the cool kids, everybody will want to be like them and copy their every move and every purchase. Got it?

Now let's set that aside and look at the other side of the aisle, which features Duncan Watts, a network-theory scientist from Columbia University with a long list of credentials. Watts's own research has found that "highly connected people are not, in fact, crucial social hubs" and that "your average slob is just as likely as a well-connected person to start a huge new trend" (see FastCompany.com, January 28, 2008, Clive Thompson). In other words, it's not about the influentials at all; to take it even further, everybody is influential and nobody is an influential. Trends will happen when they are ready to happen, not because you seeded them with people you deem to be the authority.

So what theory does Brains on Fire subscribe to? Neither, or maybe both, depending on how you look at it.

Allow us to explain.

Rather than subscribe to any sort of influencer theory, we instead subscribe to what we call the passion theory, based on a simple premise: *Influence can be made, but passion can't.* In other words, with all the tools at our disposal these days (including the almighty dollar) and with the right secret sauce, you can manufacture, build, or grow influence. But try as you may, you can't buy passion. You can't create passion. And you surely can't fake it.

"Influence can be made, but passion can't."

Geno Church – Brains on Fire,
WOM Inspiration Officer

Everywhere you look, there are white papers, books, and marketing companies based on finding and using the influencers. They tie a nice bow around the would-be concept so you can pick it up and drop it into any of your campaigns. Oh, don't get us wrong; influencer marketing has its place in word-of-mouth marketing. But it's just one way, and it's certainly not the only way. Many companies find that it's much easier to try to seed conversations with these already established so-called influencers. And while the efforts with this group might get a quick spike in attention, the buzz soon dies away—and the company is left to look for its next quick fix. Not exactly sustainable, is it? Besides, the influencers have organized themselves and now see their influence as a business, and if you're looking at it like that, then the passion and slice-of-life aspects quickly get sucked out of the equation.

Do we want to ignore those people who take up a lot of space online and have a lot of other people's attention? Of course not. We want to have conversations with them. But instead of trying to rent them like a billboard and pray that they'll talk about us, we'd rather use them for insight. So we reach out in the initial stages of igniting a movement and ask for their thoughts and opinions on how to approach the task at hand. We don't ask them to be our leaders; we don't even ask them to talk about what we're trying to do. We just talk to them about their passion. As a result, we not only gain a lot of knowledge about the industry but because of the way we approached them—by treating them like the experts they are, and without any preconceived notions—they naturally start conversations about what we are doing in an organic, authentic way.

PASSION DIAL

One of the best scenes from the mock rockumentary *This Is Spinal Tap* is when Nigel Tufnel (played by Christopher Guest) is telling Marty DiBergi (played by Rob Reiner) about his special Marshall amp head—an amp on which all dials go to 11. DiBergi asks, "Why don't you just use 10 as the loudest and make that the highest one?" and Tufnel replies, "This one goes to 11!"

Tufnel's special amp is a tribute to his passion for being the loudest band in the world. To get there, he needs one more click, one more push. And much like Nigel himself, passion is not logical. So what if we used the amp as a metaphor and asked what its equivalent within a company might be? How does passion relate to a company or an organization's customers? *Passion* is from the Latin word *patior,* meaning "to suffer or to endure." And we're sure some people would find that an accurate description of how they felt listening to Tufnel playing at 11. A more contemporary definition: "Passion is an intense emotion compelling feeling, enthusiasm or desire for anything, and often requiring action." If you want to stay with the metaphor, it's a great correlation to use when thinking about a brand's relationship with its most passionate customers. Companies should aspire to ratchet up their relationships with customers to be *one notch louder.*

Listen to what John Tanner, academic vice president at Brigham Young University, has to say on the subject:

> According to [*New York Times* columnist] Thomas Friedman, curiosity and passion are key prerequisites for education in a "flat world," where information is readily available and where global markets reward those who have learned how to learn and are self-motivated to learn. In today's world, he argues, it is more important to be passionate and curious than to be merely smart. Friedman has reduced this principle to a formula: CQ + PQ > IQ—meaning, Curiosity Quotient plus Passion

Quotient is greater than Intelligent Quotient. Friedman says that he lives by this formula: "Give me the kid with a passion to learn and a curiosity to discover and I will take him or her over the less passionate kid with a huge IQ every day of the week." IQ "still matters, but CQ and PQ . . . matter even more."

We've come to see that this formula has value for companies and organizations, specifically those that want to create long-term, sustainable movements. Passion, and not influence, should be the main driver behind the people companies choose to be internal or external ambassadors. Remember, most traditional marketers subscribe to the campaign mentality that treats customers like on-off switches, turning the marketing switch on with the start of a campaign, and when the campaign runs its multiweek course, turning it off.

But passion doesn't work like that.

Wouldn't it be preferable to treat customers as volume dials rather than on-off switches? Companies should embrace conversations that have a more sustainable long-term effect. The volume level should never go to zero, and the conversation should always continue. Sometimes it gets louder and sometimes softer, but it never ends or goes mute. There are no dark times with movements, because there is always a hum of activity.

We're using a new model for building fans these days. Musicians, for example, can control their own destiny by building a fan base through the grassroots level, social media sites and online followings. They don't have to rely on the old-school record label model. But the key to any musician's or band's success still remains the same as it ever was: the fans. Just like a company or brand's success is determined by its customers . . . and sustainable success by its fans.

Creating a real passion dial requires a company to be willing to put itself out there, and not in the anonymous sense. We mean making the internal workings and people visible and transparent to outsiders, building relationships with fans, and then recognizing the opportunities to find authentic transportation to where the fans are. For instance, bands start with vans, then go to buses, and then airplanes. They travel from their neighborhood, to cities, and then to continents.

Additionally, a band's fan growth is usually tied to performance, and the same can be said for a company. Many bands have been successful by using social media, and while that's a great way to be available to their communities of fans, it's just a small part of the equation. This scenario also requires a balance between benefiting the community—less money for the band/brand, but more loyal fans who feel a part of your journey to fame and fortune—as opposed to the sell-out, which means more money in the short term and a lot of exposure. However, it will elicit a fan base that is always looking for the next best thing, which won't necessarily be you.

Thinking this way can keep your company's efforts honest and focused on the long term. From both the fans' and the brand's perspectives, that's what we want. Marketers and brands tend to lose focus on passion too quickly, or perhaps they simply place less value on it as time goes by.

So how does a brand reach an 11 on the passion dial? You might claim that Tufnel's Marshall amp really didn't reach past 10. But if he believes it plays at 11, does it really matter whether it's actually louder? Maybe he plays his chords tighter, sustains his notes longer, and reaches 11 by feeding off the energy of his fans. That's how a brand can reach 11, when its fanatical fans infect their fanaticism into the brand's internal band members. It's easy to stop believing and just go through the motions—until you see the real value you're providing to your fans. Moving the dial from 10 to 11 cannot be done by the fans alone.

We want the 11s. We want the ones who are always going "one louder" when they're proclaiming their passion.

The nugget here is that instead of looking for those influential folks in a category, we look for those regular, everyday people who just happen to have a deep passion about that category. Not the divas, the superbloggers, or the supposed influencers that everyone else is trying to get hold of. Since most people trust the opinions of people just like themselves, why not empower those people in the first place? We've seen how these everyday people have more sway and greater credibility: because they are, in fact, "just like me."

You better believe that we look for people who have the ability to become influential and social, because a hermit who has all the passion in the world about something is still, after all, a hermit. So as we have conversations, we ask people how they relate to others, what kind of activities they're involved in, what their hobbies are, and so on. And even these "interviews" reveal a lot about their personality. Though we don't have an official psychological profile that we're targeting, there are a few obvious characteristics that we seek in our leaders.

HOW TO FIND A MOVEMENT'S LEADERS

The first thing you need to know is that if everyone is expected to lead, then no one will. The second is that the right leaders provide an inspirational tone and a context for the community that a brand simply can't accomplish on its own. So many communities are DOA because the community is built to be about the brand. But as Justine Foo puts it, "Leaders . . . re-energize that passion conversation over and over." And when you put people instead of things at the forefront of your message and movement, people look at you differently. In other words, like Scott Monty of Ford's Social Media Department says, "People appreciate having a personality associated with a company."

"If everyone is expected to lead, no one will lead."

Geno Church – Brains on Fire,
WOM Inspiration Officer

For example, the first thing we did for the Fiskars project was figure out *who* we needed to lead the movement. Now if you're not familiar with the crafting and scrapbooking world, you might assume that it's something your grandmother does. So we teamed up with Umbria Communications (now JD Power Web Intelligence), a company that dives deep into online conversation mining, to see what was being said out there, who was doing the talking, and where it was taking place. And boy, were we surprised at what they found.

First of all, our audience turned out to be members of Gen X and Gen Y—as far from your grandmother and her friends as you could imagine—and they were clearly driving the conversation. This was vital, since it helped us discover that our assumptions about the demo were way off base, and it would determine key components of the movement. Second, 25 percent of those who talked about crafting online did so *a lot*, on average, three times a week. (Yes, we're still talking about paper and scissors here.) And the last thing we found was that virtually nobody was using the Fiskars name in their conversations, so we were tasked to increase that number by 10 percent in our first four months.

Step two was about the influencers, so we began to reach out to celebrity crafters to gain their insight and input. We told them about Fiskars's intentions and the brand ambassador movement, which began to generate interest while empowering them and gaining their buy-in. It also let us identify cutting-edge crafters we could engage when we built the online and off-line tools to help authenticate the movement.

We used the conversations we had up to this point to identify the attributes we wanted in active brand ambassadors—a kind of informal psychological profile, if you will. It included personality attributes, the members of their social circles, how they connected with others online and off-line, and leadership attributes. We quickly learned from the first set of face-to-face conversations that we weren't looking for the best technical scrapbookers because those crafters only discussed that aspect of their hobby during their interview. (And keep in mind that we didn't ask them to talk about anything in particular.) However, those who weren't concerned with the technical aspect were the ones whose conversations centered on teaching, storytelling, and sharing their passion. The lightbulbs went off; these were the people we were looking for.

We were primarily looking for people we could empower to become ambassadors. While we wanted the movement's leaders to be knowledgeable and able to teach, if they were all high-level talent, then others might perceive them as unapproachable—not a good thing for a social community. Most crafters pursue this pastime as a hobby and are not highly talented, so it is easier for most to connect to someone on the same ability level.

We determined that the movement would be headed by four lead ambassadors: part-time, paid, contracted positions. We worked with Fiskars to identify four geographical markets to focus the search and interview process, and we ultimately chose Chicago, Los Angeles, Sacramento, and Charlotte.

Then we took it to the streets. We collaborated with independent crafting stores in those areas and put out an open call for interviews for the four positions. Based on the online response, candidates answered a series of short questions to help us select 75 eventual applicants for face-to-face interviews in each city. Then our team traveled the country and spent two to three days in each city, holding in-person interviews in crafting stores. This was an important component, as we wanted to talk to the applicants in their own environment, a place where they felt familiar and comfortable, much like the places where they would be interacting with fellow ambassadors.

Each candidate had her picture taken and her interview videorecorded for future reference. We simply asked each of them to bring a sampling of their scrapbooking and crafting projects with them and be prepared to talk about them. Clearly, this wasn't about sales experience or resumes or the size of the candidates' social circles. It was about passion and personality, the ability to connect, and the desire to share their enthusiasm with others. We just sat down and had a guided conversation.

We listened intently to what each woman shared with us. We knew that the leaders had to be willing to talk about their lives—the good and the bad. It's a wide boundary. If you're not comfortable with discussing your dog passing away, the issues you face in raising your kids, or even if you had a bad day, then you're not what we're looking for. And while some of the applicants merely showed us their crafting work, others showed us their work and told us the story behind it. That's what we were looking for.

After reviewing all the notes and videos, four women were chosen from four different walks of life:

- A 26-year-old single woman and former scrapbook storeowner

- A 37-year-old married mother of one who was in law enforcement and a former missionary

- A 30-year-old married mother and part-time teacher for hearing-impaired children

- A 27-year-old married stay-at-home mother

They would be the ones who would carry the torch for this movement. And in the following chapters, we tell you how.

FINDING TEEN LEADERS

The Rage against the Haze movement posed both different and similar challenges in finding our leaders. Our search led us to a woman who had received a grant from the University of South Carolina to identify kids who were doing service-based learning—from tutoring to cleanups—across the state. That gave us a great opportunity to find motivated teenagers, those who—unlike the average student—were inspired to do something more than just what they had to do to get by.

So we got in our cars and traveled the state to meet with them where they lived and were doing remarkable things—from little towns to big cities. That journey introduced us to teens who were both inspired and inspirational. It wasn't about being popular or good-looking, although some were; these kids were different. One had only been in the States for one year, and even though we could sometimes hardly understand his broken English, we always understood his passion.

We knew the movement would take every type of teen: white, black, male, female, you name it. We needed the shy ones with great artistic talent, as well as the vocal ones who couldn't draw to save their lives. Together, they created this quilt of inspiration through which Rage drew strength.

"I was never alone, and I always had people my age or a little bit older to guide me," said Chris Ivan, a member of the Rage movement from the beginning. And that's just it. They were—and still are—all in this together, to feed off and inspire one another. It's a cycle that sustains itself with the right leaders in place.

FINDING LEADERS OF A MUSICAL INSTRUMENT MOVEMENT

You'd think that when it came to finding the leaders for Best Buy's Mi11 movement that the related gear of guitars, drums, keyboards, and DJ equipment would elicit scores of rock stars. And while we do consider our leads to be rock stars, when it comes to playing a musical instrument, there are the power chords, playing on stage, and the groupies, but there's also a whole technical world as well. It's full of custom-building tube amps, choosing the right wood for the neck of your guitar, and finding the combination of pedals that gives you just the right amount of fuzz. Let's face it, not all of us who enjoy playing our guitars are exactly rock stars (well, maybe in our own heads). So we had to make sure that our leaders had the chops to relate on a variety of levels. We could have just chosen the trendy ones, but as sexy as that might be, it's not reality. So we identified and chose approachable people who were also storytellers, people who could relate to someone who was about to pick up a guitar for the first time, as well as someone who'd been playing drums for years. That was the balance we wanted to find.

As Eric Dodds, the "Community Guy" for the Mi11 movement, put it:

> The leads are what make this thing. It wouldn't work without them. They come from a variety of backgrounds; have a variety of expertise in each of their quivers; and [collectively] make up one of the most awesome music resources in the country. They were already doing entrepreneurial things to promote musical instruments at Best Buy. We are just giving them a channel and resources to do that [as a group] and invite others to [do it as well].

Best Buy's corporate offices reiterate this claim. "We have a really unique retail culture here. We wanted people that were good representatives of that," says Jamie Plesser.

GROWING INFLUENCE CREATES LOYALTY

Here's the beautiful thing: When you take the time to recognize someone and empower them with the tools they need to pass on the word, they will be much more loyal to you than the mommy blogger who is basically renting out her influence to the highest bidder and will be talking about something else in a matter of days.

Some people think they'll have it made if only Oprah will talk about them. But Oprah is going to talk about somebody different tomorrow. And the next day. And the next. And soon you'll be left on the shelf next to what she touted the day before your product. Oh, we have no doubt that you'll get a bump in sales and ride that wave as far as it takes you. But it's temporary.

In our experience—which is not driven by charts, data, or statistics but rather by hands-on experience—success comes when you give power to those who have the potential to influence others. It isn't always the coolest people or the giants in an industry, but they aren't unconnected slobs, either. It's the everyday people we've seen become influencers. They have risen in the communities they serve and have, in turn, raised others in the community as well. So now they are influencers making influencers. And so it spreads.

Authors and experts like Watts, Keller, and Gladwell are all great thinkers who have most definitely influenced our efforts to ignite sustainable movements and fuse them into the very core of brand identities. The only thing we have had to go on, though, is hands-on, frontline experience and our gut, both of which have served us well.

It's both great for the word-of-mouth marketing industry and healthy for all of us that there isn't only one camp to pull from. So as the debate rages on and both sides generate more data to support their views, we have no doubt that we'll all benefit from their thinking—or at least get some more reading that'll make your head hurt.

PASSIONATE PEOPLE PUT IN THE HARD WORK

Rob Morris from Love146 gave us this nugget of insight in one of our discussions: "Will influencers give you sweat equity? No. But the *passionate* ones will."

In our experience, we've found that over time, influencers come to expect you to bring things to them. They sit back and start to get lax. They're influencers, after all. We should all listen to them, right? But the passionate folks—the ones who aren't afraid to roll up their sleeves and be a part of something bigger than themselves—are happy to contribute sweat equity, something that goes far beyond tweeting or blogging about something. Sweat equity is a personal sacrifice. When you give you sweat equity, you give your loyalty. Your time. Your effort.

And we'd take 100 passionate people who contribute that sweat equity just because they care, as opposed to 1,000 influentials who tweet once and never think about it again.

REMEMBER, IT TAKES ONLY ONE

All it takes is one person to start a movement. That's right, one person. Not 100 influencers, not 50 bloggers, and not 1,000 ambassadors. One. Passionate. Person. That's all it takes.

But that one person has to be committed. They have to not care what others think, and they have enough fervor that they can do their own thing. And once they are out there, giving it all they've got, they can't help attracting kindred spirits who join the cause and start giving it all they've got as well.

In 2009, there was a great video that was randomly taped at the Sasquatch Music Festival. In it, a normal (and kinda goofy) guy got up in the field and started dancing (or maybe flailing around) to the music being played on stage. Some people laughed. Some people pointed. Some just sat and watched. Pretty soon, he was joined by an equally goofy guy who jumped up and started dancing with him. Then another. Then a few others. And within three minutes, people were sprinting to join the dance party. Hundreds of them. Do you think the guy who started the whole thing was an influencer? Or just someone who *had* to do his thing?

QUIET LEADERS

The people you need to look to for igniting your movement may not be the people you originally thought of. They might even be the quiet leaders. And as this whole word-of-mouth marketing thing keeps growing and evolving—especially with the rise of social media—we often overlook the quiet leader.

Quiet leaders let their actions speak louder than anyone's words ever could. People watch them intently, and they don't really know why. There is strength in their silence, and they choose their actions deliberately.

Quiet leaders leave ego by the wayside. They understand that ego is a powerful, ugly beast that can easily take over a typical influencer's life, and when it does, they're no longer leaders. Just noise.

Quiet leaders elevate those around them instead of always trying to elevate themselves. And when you elevate others, they never forget it. They are loyal. They are always happy to return the gesture.

When we were searching for leaders for Rage against the Haze, one of our most active and effective teens actually found us. Zack was a quintessential quiet leader. Both of his parents smoked, and his goal was to get his mother to quit. But in getting involved, he found that he had a voice. This guy was six-foot three and 15 years old, and he wore button-down shirts with pocket protectors every day—certainly not the type of guy to stand on top of a van and lead chants. Instead, he was having quiet conversations with kids who were struggling with the same issues he was. He was warm and approachable, and he is the perfect example of the assertion that it takes a lot of different kinds of people to move something forward. Zack was always there. He always showed up and was always the last one to leave.

On his last day with the movement, before he aged out of it and went off to college, Zack was having lunch at a Rage event in downtown Greenville. All the teens were going around the table reminiscing about the summer and about Rage events all over the state. When it came to Zack's turn, he couldn't say a word, because he was overcome with emotion. All these other teens, from all walks of life and all social groups, gathered around him and hugged him. That's the kind of emotion that you can't get from a campaign, and that's the kind of passion that brings us together.

So don't forget the silent leaders. They just might be the ones you've been overlooking, and they could very well be the key to your success. There could be one answering the phones at the front desk. Maybe there's one in the accounting department, or down in shipping. You never know until you start to listen to what others are saying and start to dig in and see where people are getting their input and information. Because in this case—even though it may be counterintuitive—silence is indeed golden.

BUT I WANT ONLY THE COOL, SEXY PEOPLE TO BE THE LEADERS OF MY MOVEMENT

Then you're going to have to move your company to dreamland, because that's where your head is right now.

"Diversity of leaders is important. It creates a quilt of inspiration."

Geno Church – Brains on Fire,
WOM Inspiration Officer

Listen very closely: You cannot choose the people who will love your company. It's not up to you to do the choosing; it's up to them. People come in every shape, size, and color. They come from different backgrounds and espouse different belief systems. If you pick your leaders for their appearance, you're doomed. Because unless you're in the high-fashion model industry, that's not reality. It takes all kinds, and passion comes in a lot of different packages. So learn to deal with it now.

Movements Have a Barrier of Entry

There's a supposedly secret driving track in the Southeastern United States where BMW tests new concept cars. It's a pretty nondescript place, but the earth is raised around the edges, and bushes and trees have been planted along the hills to obscure the track. And then, of course, there's the 12-foot chain-link fence topped with spiraled razor-sharp barbed wire. Seeing the Keep Out signs posted up and down the fence, anyone who drives by begins to wonder what's in there. What are they trying to keep you from seeing? What's the big secret?

Those of us who are naturally curious immediately want to know. We'll drive around the entire perimeter and strain our necks to see if we can get a glimpse. It's exclusive. It's top secret. And if only we could see something, then, boy, would we have a story to tell. The barrier of entry is calling us to want to know what we don't know.

One of the secret sauces we've discovered in igniting movements is that a barrier of entry is vital. Yes, we *want* to keep people out of the movement; in fact, it's a key to success, growth, and sustainability.

How many social networking sites do you belong to on the Internet? You know: FaceBook, Twitter, LinkedIn, message boards, blogs, brand communities, and the like. Now, how many do you visit on a regular basis? Better yet, how many have to you gone to, signed up (as in gone to the "create account" page where you create a user name and password), looked around for a few clicks, and then never gone back? If you're anything like the rest of the world, we're guessing the answer is a lot. Dozens even. There is no barrier of entry there, so it's easy to sign up, look around, leave, and never think about it again. There's no wall, no gatekeeper, and no reason we should really be all that curious about these sites and whatever they're trying to get us to sign up for. The Internet is littered with dead communities whose sign-up portion we guarantee someone worked long and hard to make as quick and painless as possible. We're not saying that's the only thing that killed them, but it didn't help any, that's for sure.

How many newsletters and e-mail blasts do you get in your in-box on a daily basis that you signed up for once upon a time, but now drag and drop into your junk folder or just plain delete? Why would you want to sign up for junk?

So how did we figure out the importance of barriers to entry? By chance. The client for Rage against the Haze—the South Carolina Department of Environmental Health and Control (DHEC)—made us build a barrier of entry as part of their program because of the legal complications of getting information from minors. The fact that the DHEC wouldn't let us allow kids to just go sign up forced us to think differently.

Because of the nature of what they do—and what they need to control—the DHEC was very concerned about kids attacking the tobacco industry on their own. South Carolina is a tobacco-producing state, after all, so not just anybody can go out there and shout for Rage. It would have been devastating to our client, because they ultimately report to the state legislature, and the state legislature needs to look out for the tobacco farmers. So, like it or not (and we didn't), we had to put a barrier of entry in place. And although we were against it, we didn't realize that this meant that we trusted our fans to do the right thing early on. We could educate and empower them, but in the end, it was on them to use that knowledge in the way they saw fit.

One guaranteed method of figuring out an alternate means to accomplishing your goals is to have an obstacle placed in your path. Rage was allowed to have members, but prospective members had to go through a process. They weren't permitted to simply register; we built the program that way because we had no choice. It worked as a two-way street, though; they were checking us out to see if they wanted to be a part of this movement, and we were checking them out as well.

When we were recruiting leaders for the Park Angels of Charleston movement, we directed interested people to a web site where they could fill out an application. A *long* application. It had dozens of pieces of information to fill in, as well as deep, open-ended questions about applicants' beliefs and how they would handle certain situations. It probably took a solid couple of hours to complete. About a week into the process, we noticed that many people were abandoning the application at about the halfway mark. Someone who was new in the office blurted out the question, "What's happening? The application is too long! Nobody's finishing!" But being a leader of the Park Angels was a volunteer position. If someone wasn't going to dedicate two hours to fill out the application, what would make us think that they were going to stick with the entire program? We wanted dedication, commitment, and perseverance, and this was a great way to determine if an individual possessed those qualities.

Another example is the process of becoming a Fiskateer. The way to join the movement—whether you've stumbled on the site or heard about it via word of mouth—is simply to ask. A visit to the web site (www.fiskateers.com) allows a potential applicant to read about the program, find out what's involved, and learn about the movement's four or five different leaders. Applicants can then choose whichever leader to whom they feel most connected and send the leader an e-mail saying they'd like to become a Fiskateer. They'll usually receive an e-mail back within 24 hours. Some of them are canned responses, and some of them are personal, depending on who the leader is and how much time she has to respond. Basically, that e-mail says, "That's so great that you want to join the Fiskateer movement. Can you tell me why?"

We lose more than 50 percent of the so-called interested people right there. And we think that's fantastic. Again, if that person isn't willing to send an e-mail back with *any* reason at all— from "My sister told me about it" to "I hear you get sneak peeks" to "I love crafting"—then the odds are that they aren't going to be an active member of the community. Active members are the ones who engage others, create content, answer questions, and put skin in the game. And that's all we're asking from the get-go: to put a little skin in the game. It must be give and take.

AND HERE COMES THE QUANTITY VERSUS QUALITY DEBATE

We can hear it now: "But a barrier of entry keeps people out. And I want a *lot* of people to join my movement. Because if I have 500,000 people join my community, then maybe I can get at least 2 percent of those people to be active. That's still 10,000 people. And that's a lot. Right?"

Sure it is. But you're going to have to drop a lot of cash on getting those half-million people to pay attention to you and actually sign up. We're talking a hefty spend. And if you have it and want to spend it, then more power to you.

But what if you had a community of 5,000 people—75 percent of whom were active? What if you knew that every time you asked the community to help you with a survey, you would receive triple the participation rates of your competition? Quality trumps quantity, and as the vice president of brand marketing at Fiskars, Jay Gillespie, told us, "For me, it's not about the numbers. It's about growing even deeper relationships." In other words, he'd rather concentrate on building meaningful connections with the members who are already part of the movement. And as that happens, more people will naturally be attracted to it.

"For me, it's not about the numbers. It's about growing even deeper relationships."

Jay Gillespie – Fiskars, Vice President of Brand Marketing

By laying the foundation with those who choose to put some skin in the game, you're building sustainability. These people care about the success of the movement. They are taking personal ownership, and by doing so, they elevate everything—and everyone—else. It's not about the company, brand, or product anymore. It's not about you. It's about "us."

When you throw open your organization's doors and do the cattle call, you devalue everything you worked so hard for. You're absolutely free, and you don't require any effort or time to join—and *free* will cause people to come out of the woodwork. *Free* stops people in their tracks and immediately gets their attention. And the thing is, no matter what it is, if it's free, people will take one of those, please. Case in point: After a local 5K run was a tent that provided the usual postrace staples: water, bananas, and sports drinks. Oh, and two huge boxes that everyone was grabbing these plastic pouches from. What was in the pouch? Some sort of tablet that you put in your washing machine to make it smell better. Do you really think your washing machine smells funny? It didn't matter to the people that were there; it was free, so they took one. Some people took three, even.

But when you're creating any kind of program, movement, or gathering of people around your brand, you're setting the stage for disaster if you build it on *free*. For example, "Sign up for our ambassador program and receive two free coupons for a free meal!" Or "Join our Brand X Club and get a free pair of X!"

We see it over and over again. Why disaster? Because—just like the donkey—if you dangle that free carrot in front of someone, he or she will do the minimal amount of work required to get the prize. And then it's done. At least until you dangle another carrot. There are *huge* message boards solely dedicated to how to get free stuff. And many of your word-of-mouth companies and programs are in those posts. People are actually sharing with one another what the minimal amount of work they have to do to get something free from you . . . and then they're gone. No thank-you, and certainly no loyalty.

Free should be used as a random act of kindness. And if you do try to build something on free, then put up enough barriers to make sure people are joining for the right reasons. Because free can sabotage everything you try to do, right out of the gate.

That goes for giving out swag for free, too. (SWAG stands for "Stuff We All Get," like T-shirts, bags, and stickers.) Back in 2001, The Truth campaign and most state-led teen anti-tobacco campaigns were based on making villains of the tobacco industry and giving away tons of free swag. Who could blame them? The tobacco settlement funds infused state budgets from Minnesota to Florida. Those were heydays for advertising agencies, and teens loaded up on swag from shirts to dashboard fuzzy dice.

Considering the power that South Carolina's tobacco industry held, we felt that our strategy for Rage against the Haze had to be quite a bit different. But to be honest, we didn't get it right the first time, either. Our initial effort—a 30-day street marketing tour of the state—was filled with successes and some failures. We learned from both and, as a result, created some important rules:

1. Go where the party is already happening. Don't create your own party and expect people to show up. Staging your own event in a rural town like Walterboro, South Carolina, sounds like a great idea, but if all the teens in town hang out at Wal-Mart, you're going to be more successful hanging out at Wal-Mart, too. This also is what led us to create Friday Night Rage four years ago. If you want to go to the party on an autumn Friday night in South Carolina, you can just about choose any high school football game in the state—and the whole town will be there.

2. Include your audience in creating the message. The Rage teens felt it was important for the first Rage swag to have the South Carolina state flag prominent. Why? Because they believed that the state motto, *Dum spero spiro* (While I Breathe, I Hope) was a contradiction, and it was a story they felt empowered to tell.

3. Be brave enough to tell some folks that the message is not for them. Our Rage teens considered this to be the most important aspect of Rage swag. No adults would be allowed to get it or wear it—which did make for some awkward moments. Adults seemed to feel more entitled to swag than teens, but the movement wasn't about adults, and our participants wanted people to remember that.

4. Just because it's free doesn't mean people want it or, for that matter, that they'll wear it. Free baggy T-shirts with a big giant logo across the chest aren't going to get your message seen. The more Rage moved away from pushing logos and moved to messages (like "I Love My Lungs"), the more teens wanted them. We have a tradition of slingshotting T-shirts during halftime at football games. One teen even bought a Rage shirt for $20 off another teen.

5. Engage in hand-to-hand combat. We hate making a purchase in a store where the person taking our money doesn't even give us the courtesy of a thank-you. So why do people sit behind a table at an event and just point to the free stuff for you to take? Rage teens made every interaction an opportunity, and they called it "hand-to-hand combat." It usually started with a handshake, and slipping a camo rubber band bracelet on the unsuspecting wrist.

The deeper the conversations, the more valuable the swag exchange, because swag created the right way lives on past that initial conversation. That goes for joining a community as well. The deeper the relationships from the very beginning, the more value a person gets from that community. In turn, it makes it a lot more likely that they will add to the community, therefore creating more content and value for others. It's a beautiful circle.

EXCLUSIVITY

The other great thing about having a barrier of entry is the air of exclusivity it creates. Having a movement that has that barrier as opposed to one that doesn't is the difference between the secret clubhouse and the mall.

When we're invited to become members of the secret club, we of course want to tell others about it. It makes us feel good about ourselves. But we're careful who we tell. We don't want just anyone to come to the secret meetings—only people we deem worthy. So now you're not only feeling ownership, you're feeling empowered. You feel authorized to do the recruiting because, as a member, you feel like you need to pick and choose the other members to maintain the integrity of the club. It's your job. You're the gatekeeper now.

BARRIER OF ENTRY AS A RELATIONSHIP BUILDER

As Alex Wipperfurth and John Grant write in their white paper "How Cults Seduce," the Jehovah's Witness group has a fascinating way of recruiting new members into the church. The first time you are visited by recruiters, two people come to your door. But the next time they come, one is someone who wasn't there for your previous visit. They do this three times. Each time they show up, you know one of them and you don't know the other.

That means that by the time you decide to visit the church, you know at least four people who are members. Putting up a barrier of entry for the Fiskateers achieved the same effect. Since the only way to join the movement is through one of the leaders, there was an automatic relationship established, and you knew at least one person when you entered into the community.

The problem with the vast majority of communities—online and off—is that the bigger they are, the more chance you have of getting lost in the shuffle. Large churches are a great example of this. Yes, they have databases and welcome committees and greeters and are doing just about everything they can to make sure visitors don't slip through the cracks unnoticed, but people still do.

When you already know at least one person there, you have a connection. You have a reason to come back. And most important, you have someone to talk to. It's a cutting technique, and giving a little bit of your effort, time, money, and reputation can be a vital part of that barrier.

LESSON #5

Movements Empower People with Knowledge

"It's time to open the kimono."

It's a set of words that Brains on Fire founder Mike Goot used frequently, and it brings a vivid image to your mind, doesn't it? It's meant to. All it means is that you need to let your fans see what's underneath all the formality. Go ahead and reveal what's under the makeup, done-up hair, and fancy, shiny clothing.

Are you scared that they'll find out that you're not perfect? We have a feeling they already know that. Listen, admitting your mistakes makes you human. And people love to know that companies are human—or at least made up of humans. Nobody's perfect, and when you pretend to be, people resent you for it and go to extreme measures to point out that you are, in fact, flawed, not to mention it also makes you look ignorant.

So when you mess up, consider an apology. Apologies are powerful. And sometimes they make those who already love you love you even more, not to mention help some others who weren't sure about you get off that fence and join the fans.

But we digress . . .

Your fans want to know everything about you and your industry, the good stuff and especially the bad stuff. We all know that knowledge is power, and people love to let other people know that they have a secret to share: the inside scoop, the bumps and bruises. Your customers want you to expose yourself, put it all out there for the world to see. Sure, this scares the hell out of most companies, because they don't want to divulge their screwups and mistakes. But that's reality. Companies are made up of people, and people are fallible. The ones who admit this win.

And the great thing about knowledge is that it spreads, organically and naturally, and inside knowledge spreads even more rapidly. It's an entry point and an opportunity to form a deeper relationship; it can create a bond and provide common ground. And sharing it is vital to igniting a movement.

Because knowledge is power, when you give your fans knowledge, you're empowering them. It's a key element to any movement, and there are several ways to go about it.

GOOD magazine's Ligaya Mishan wrote an article on the rising popularity of 1920s-style speakeasy restaurants. Yes, secret restaurants in cities all over the world that survive completely on word of mouth. Let's put aside for a moment the fact that there are no check-ins with fire marshals or sanitary code people, shall we? Instead, let's talk about the mysterious nature of these eateries.

It's human nature to want to be in the know. From the secret decoder rings some of us craved as kids to that friend who works at your favorite company and lets you in on a top-secret revolutionary product that is yet to be released, secrets are powerful. Even better, secrets are power. As one of the chefs in Mishan's article says, "This is not about the food. I can tell you lots of places with better food." It is, however, about the experience of knowing something that most others don't know and about getting together with a handful of people who *do* know.

So how can companies share secrets that benefit everyone? (In a non-FCC violating way, of course.) How can you open your company's kimono to those who love you? Why are you keeping all those juicy tidbits to yourself? And if you do decide to share a secret, how can you do it in such a way that you're not divulging information that obviously is trying to drive sales but is also trying to build advocates?

EMPOWERING TEENAGERS ISN'T ROCKET SCIENCE

After finding our original 92 leaders for Rage against the Haze, we needed to empower them with knowledge. The ubiquitous TRUTH campaign that was currently running ads in several states was approaching the situation by building fear and hatred of the tobacco industry. You might remember the body bags or the cowboy singing out of the artificial voice box in his neck because of his throat cancer. There were even TV spots with teens in the streets in front of a tobacco company's headquarters with bullhorns and protests.

As we mentioned in Chapter 4, because South Carolina is a tobacco-producing state, we had limitations placed on us from the beginning, one of which was that we could not vilify the tobacco industry. We couldn't even say "Big Tobacco" because of the negative connotations it carried. So while we couldn't be anti-tobacco, we could be anti–tobacco use. It might be semantics, but it's reality.

We quickly realized that restrictions on our communications necessitated a path that wasn't based on fear and anger. So we decided to inform with law, science, and finding each individual's own voice in the movement. That would be our education arm for Rage against the Haze.

We gathered together our 92 teens from all over South Carolina for a weekend of intense learning—with a whole lot of fun and bonding built in as well. Since then, it's become a staple of the movement that happens at least once a year, but now it's our current leaders who are teaching the newcomers. We've taken adults out of the equation so that it's completely peer to peer.

The existing model in other states for a movement like Rage was to host some form of summer retreat and bring in a bunch of people to discuss the effects of tobacco use and media literacy and tobacco companies lying to you, give you some stuff, and send you on your way. However, we decided to do something different, because while that model had a "mountain-top experience," it wasn't sustainable. We wondered if we could instead create a curriculum that teens could use to train other teens. By putting them in charge—rather than introducing an adult to "teach" like they were used to and bored with—they would feel a much greater sense of ownership.

So Ragefest was born. Although we did bring in some adults, the intention was simply to arm the teens with useful and usable information. One was a brain addiction specialist who broke down the ways in which nicotine affects the human body. Another was one of the lawyers who played a key role in suing the tobacco companies over the bogus nature of "light" cigarettes. Another speaker was a trauma doctor who explained why people end up in the emergency room with heart attacks from smoking. These were real people on the front lines; they didn't talk down to the teens and instead gave them bite-size pieces of information that the leaders could actually use. In addition, the teens got more involved and wanted to know more specific things—because now they were gathering information they could really use to approach their loved ones about their tobacco use.

We also brought in some MTV celebrities at the time—like Yes Duffy and Oscar Hernandez—whose job it was to show the teens how to use their own gifts to create their voice for the movement. These guests encouraged them to tap into talents and interests like art, poetry, writing, and music to bring other people to the mission. There wasn't just a single way to go about it; there were several. And that realization led those 92 leaders to respect one another. They came to see that the movement wasn't just about an individual voice, but rather about caring for one another. And that is a major component to their success.

Our teens also used their own experiences to teach each another about street marketing. We established a rule early on that we were not there to make people feel bad about their own

tobacco use. In other words, we were never anti–tobacco user—
a message hammered home by the teens themselves. Quentin
James, one of the original Rage leaders, explains:

> We were 14- and 15-year-olds who were basically given
> a location and tools . . . we created the ideas, campaigns,
> strategies, way to talk with people, and we taught our
> teams how to do it ourselves. To be able to go to a small
> city, get kids together, train them, [and] give them the
> inspiration and the tools to lead a movement forward . . .
> that was phenomenal.

"To be able to go to a small city, get kids together, train them, give them the inspiration and the tools to lead a movement forward. That was phenomenal."

Quentin James – Rage Against The Haze,
One of the original 92 Teen Leaders
in South Carolina's Anti-tobacco Movement

Our purpose was not to spread hate; it was to empower with
knowledge and build a curriculum based on finding one's own
voice, gravitating to one's own message, and then using one's
own talents—whether freestyle rapping or public speaking—to
spread that message.

The curriculum we penned for Rage in 2002 laid the foundation for every movement we helped ignite down the road. While
each of them is custom-designed, there are recurring themes
in each, which you can see in the following tale about how we
empowered the Fiskateers with knowledge.

PASSION IN MADISON

We like to create a "come to Mecca" experience for each training session. In this case, it happened to be Fiskars U.S. Headquarters in Madison, Wisconsin, and while that might not seem like much of a Mecca for you and me, for crafters, this is where the magic happens. They didn't see the gray cube farms. Instead, they saw a place where new products go from idea to production. They saw a whole building dedicated to their passion. This serves as a great reminder that it's always a good idea to see things through your customers' eyes. Bringing the four leaders to the Fiskars headquarters helped them realize that they were now an important part of the company who were valued for their insight and input.

"We dig deep into who the leads are as people."

Eric Dodds – Best Buy Mill Community Guy
talking about the curriculum

The empowering curriculum sessions were broken down into the following parts:

DNA

We wanted the Fiskateers to dig deep and learn about the unique qualities and strengths they were bringing to the table. So using the skills with which they were so comfortable, they scrapped mini-albums exploring those attributes. We created the session to show them that they were all chosen for some common reasons but also brought distinctive talents to the movement that the others didn't. We wanted them to see that some of them were stronger on-line and some were stronger off-line. We wanted to let them know that they all had unique personalities and backgrounds and, because of that, they wouldn't always agree on everything—and that was okay. They needed to know that their voice was important, since we had different people leading this thing with different backgrounds, belief systems, cultures, and life experiences. We wanted them to connect and bring others to the movement. Remember, it takes all kinds. Not only did this help get everyone on the same page; it helped them build respect for one another and unify the four leaders.

It also set the stage for the leads to show the way when it came to setting a tone in the community for respect. As one of the leads said, "There are bound to be disagreements, but in the end we all love each other and come together." Without having to mandate respect, this was the kind of attitude we were aiming for.

We took this concept and altered it a bit for Best Buy's Mi11 movement for musical instruments. The Mi11 community guy, Eric Dodds, explains it this way: "For example, we presented the leads with an object and asked, 'What is the first memory that comes up from your childhood?' We dug deep into who they were as a person."

" What was more important was the bonding that took place outside the formal training."

Jamie Plesser – Best Buy
Marketing Strategy and Communication

It's hugely important that the movement's leads get to know what makes the others tick. Best Buy's Jamie Plesser explains his viewpoint: "For me what was more important was the bonding that took place outside the formal training agenda. They didn't really know each other before then, yet they had so much in common they seemed like a group of people that you could see being friends."

Scrap U

This session was a history lesson about Fiskars. However, we didn't want to present a slideshow with a lame voiceover about how scissors are made. We're talking about a 360-year-old company born in Finland that started out making plows and now makes an array of different products, including the iconic (and trademarked) orange-handled scissors. Those same scissors you use on a daily basis are actually in the New York Museum of Modern Art. Yes, a pair of scissors. See? There's a lot you never knew about a scissor company. And while a lot of you don't care, think about a brand that helps you participate in your passion, no matter what it might be. What if you had a wealth of knowledge about that company?

The lesson gave the leads stories to tell about the company and allowed them to see it as more than a scissor manufacturer. Ford's Scott Monty agrees that involvement has to go beyond content. "Everybody talks about content, but it's more than content. It comes down to storytelling. And without the compelling story and the compelling storyteller, you're going to get lost in the mass."

Not only did the leads learn about the company and its products but they learned from and had an audience with the executive suite. Fiskars's director of public relations and vice president of marketing delivered the intimate lesson and answered questions. The four leads couldn't believe they were in the same room with high-level execs who took time out to prepare and deliver this section of the curriculum. Again, this empowered them with knowledge of the company and showed them how valued they were.

"It's more than content. It comes down to storytelling."

Scott Monty – Ford Motor Company,
Head of Social Media

Infection

This session gave us the chance to share the notion of idea viruses with the leads and discuss ways ideas spread from one person to the next, both online and off. This is by far the most in-depth section of all.

We first teach them how to blog. This conversation starts out something like this: "Don't you *dare* go on that blog and say things like 'Fiskars is the best. I love Fiskars. Everyone should go out and buy Fiskars products right now.'" The truth is that no crafter has just Fiskars products in their crafting arsenal; they have all different brands. In fact, we said, let's start out not even talking about tools. (Reframing the conversation, remember?) Instead, we taught the leaders to blog about their lives. If their kid threw up in the back seat on the way to school, we wanted them to blog about it. If they went to a neighbor's cocktail party, blog about it. Had a good day or a bad day? Tell us why and blog about it. In other words, let your life and personality shine through, because that's how people are going to connect with you. And guess what? If you talk about your lives, then you'll necessarily talk about your passions. So crafting would naturally work its way into the conversation.

Then we asked them to be honest when it was appropriate for them to talk about products. If they didn't like a Fiskars product, we wanted them to blog about it. If they liked a competitor's product more than one of Fiskars's, then they could blog about it. And after we picked the lawyers up off the ground, Fiskars showed their true courage and desire to strive to be better and encourage that conversation.

Transparency is a cornerstone of any successful movement. So this point is hammered home in all of the curricula we develop— no more so than when the leads of the movement are part-time employees. As one of our leads put it so plainly in the training: "I am a crafter first. And I'm a Fiskars employee second." What a great statement! As you've read in previous chapters, we searched for those who were truly passionate and love to share that passion with others. Once we identified that passion, then we hired the leads for Fiskars. In the case with Rage against the Haze and the Park Angels, the leads are *not* paid, so the formula can work in both cases.

On Paying Your Lead Ambassadors

We realize the potential controversy that accompanies the idea of paying ambassadors. But if they are truly ambassadors, then the pay is just a bonus. We don't pay people to push product. But when you're asking for someone's time— sometimes more than 20 hours a week—without giving them anything in return, then it's hard to hold people accountable. The lead Fiskateers had weekly, monthly, and yearly requirements to fulfill in terms of the number of times they blogged, how many off-line events they coordinated, and so on. You get the idea. First of all, we were asking a lot. And second, believe us, they don't get paid a lot. It *has* to be a passion when you're asked for 20 hours a week and you're giving 30 or 40.

Returning to transparency, we taught the leads to always, always, *always* sign their names and identify themselves as a lead Fiskateer when answering any questions or commenting on other web sites, message boards, or blogs. No exceptions, ever. With the IZEA model (pay per post and sponsored tweets) and even models like BzzAgent, it's hard—really, impossible—to hold hundreds of thousands of people accountable for transparency. But it's very doable—and enforceable—with four or five or even a dozen people. And requiring the leads to be transparent in every interaction naturally trickled down into the rest of the strictly volunteer community. Thousands of Fiskateers were signing their names and Fiskateer affiliation on blog posts, comments, message boards, photos, and galleries, and that is a beautiful thing.

How to Be an Ambassador

Come in closely and listen to this one: We do *not* teach the leaders in the movements we ignite how to sell or how to be sales reps. They will never be held accountable for sales figures and never carry a sales sheet, nor will they be asked to pimp product or conduct sales visits with retail store owners. If they did, they would have been hired by the sales department, and their title would be "sales representative" or "sales associate." And that's not the reason they were found, hired, and trained. They are ambassadors.

So now since we know what an ambassador isn't, let's talk about what it is. First of all, here's what the dictionary defines as an *ambassador*:

noun
1. a diplomatic official of the highest rank, sent by one sovereign or state to another as its resident representative (ambassador extraordinary and plenipotentiary).
2. a diplomatic official of the highest rank sent by a government to represent it on a mission, as for negotiating a treaty.
3. a diplomatic official serving as permanent head of a country's mission to the United Nations or some other international organization.
4. an authorized messenger or representative.

That's all well and good; but our definition goes a lot deeper. Not only do we believe that a brand ambassador is an individual who is especially passionate for a particular service or product;

we believe that a brand ambassador is a loyal and loud advocate who spreads goodwill in the name of that company, product, or service. It is a dedicated mission that is personal and fulfilling for that person. They are *not* there for PR or to push product, but to spread the love.

An ambassador is a messenger of goodwill. That's the job, and the job is their passion. But don't take our word for it.

The Life of a Brand Ambassador, by Stephenie Hamen, Fiskateer #003

Two years ago, I found myself searching for some information on the Fiskars web site when I saw an icon off to the side that said, "Become a Fiskars Brand Warrior." Now, as a crafter and avid fan of their product, my curiosity was piqued. I clicked on [the icon]; and my life has never been the same.

Soon after I applied online, I had my face-to-face interview with the staff at Brains on Fire and was subsequently hired for a groundbreaking program in the crafting industry— the Fiskateers. Four women who love to craft and scrap from across the country were hired, and I am one of them. I felt like I had won the lottery [the day I got that call].

To totally understand why I was so excited to be working as a Brand Ambassador for Fiskars, I explained it to my husband—who is a golfer—like this: Ping [a company that makes golf equipment] is going to hire you to go out and play golf. They are going to provide you with all the latest and greatest products; and each time they come up with something new, you get that, too. You just go and golf. You don't have to be good, or even keep score. You just have to love the game. They are also going to give you stuff to give away to other golfers to try and keep and use. They are going to pay for all of this golf, fly you to play golf in other states, and they are also going to give you a paycheck . . . would you turn that down?

For those of us who do this, it is not a job. It is a passion. I don't sell products, no matter what anyone thinks or says. We sell nothing, because we are not sales reps. I am a crafter first and a Fiskars employee second. They have never [told] us to say we like something we don't. They have asked our honest opinion of ideas and products so many times it would scare most other companies. They have let us voice our concerns about products on the blog and publicly. They have never censored our responses or our thoughts. They have made changes to products based on our feedback as a community. They let us share the bad along with the good. They have brought us in and made us part of their team, but not in a way that compromises our thoughts, ideas, or art. We are able to post projects and ideas using products other than Fiskars and are not limited to just their tools and consumable lines. How many companies do you know would do that? I don't know of many, but this works—and it works well!

There is something about Fiskars allowing us to take some ownership of their company that has people worldwide proudly sporting and showing off their one-of-a-kind engraved scissors. They are a company that not only listens to but embraces their customers, artists, crafters, and creative minds from every walk of life.

I live and breathe this program. Hundreds of people have thanked us for being the first truly positive, open, and inviting crafting site on the web. Newcomers never feel shunned; [they] are welcomed in with open arms. First-time scrappers are not

(continued)

(Continued)

afraid to post their work as they are on other sites, because we raise people up and encourage them here. The point of this whole movement is to inspire people to share their love of crafting and . . . their passion for creating, no matter what their medium, skill level, or talent. And, even at thousands of members, it still feels like a small, friendly, close-knit [group].

It is about building community. It is about learning from each other. It is about inspiring people to try something new. It is about friendship. It is about crafters and scrappers coming together.

While it is sponsored and supported by Fiskars, at the end of the day, it belongs to us. All of us. I am proud to be Fiskateer #003, a number I wear with pride. I wear my orange shoes, my orange shirts, my apron, and my love of this community everywhere I go. This is not a job, it is a way of life, a passion, a dedication, and a commitment to bring crafters together.

This is the life of a Fiskars Brand Ambassador—a life that I wouldn't trade for the world.

Bring It Home

In this final session, we always want to make sure that the leads know that while all this new information was great, it doesn't mean anything if they can't take it home and apply it in their real lives. This session was designed to explore those concerns and help the rubber meet the road when they return to their separate sections of the country.

In a lot of such training, companies gather fans together and give them a mountaintop experience that is enjoyable but not exactly sustainable. When those fans go back home, they're on fire. But as the days and weeks progress, they ease back into their lives and that mountaintop high fades away. So we designed this section of the curriculum to sustain that feeling and encourage action. To keep the movement, well, moving. The program's success is not at the headquarters of the company; it takes place in small towns and big towns, face-to-face, all across the country. That's where it has to live and breathe: on a local level. That's the lifeblood of a movement.

The curriculum for Best Buy's Mi11 movement followed the same outline but was devised to speak the language of people who were passionate about helping others find their "music inside." The training started out with a list of introspective questions, such as "If you could bring three foods with you to a desert island to eat for the rest of your life, what would they be?"

That led to more revealing questions, like the kind of books participants love and which movies have influenced them. Then we go even deeper. For example, we'd present them with an object and ask them the first memory that comes up from their childhood—all to help them remember and then share with the others who they are as persons and what makes them tick.

The result? At the end of the first day together—even though you've just met these people that you've exchanged some e-mails and talked on the phone with—you walk out of the room knowing about their passions, hopes, and fears. You really see them as individuals, not employees or colleagues, but people.

At its most basic level, the curriculum teaches our leaders how to create fans by spreading their passion. We call this the fan cycle.

THE FAN CYCLE

The fan cycle is a series of steps that provide a blueprint for turning passive participation into ownership for a brand, product, service,

FAN CYCLE

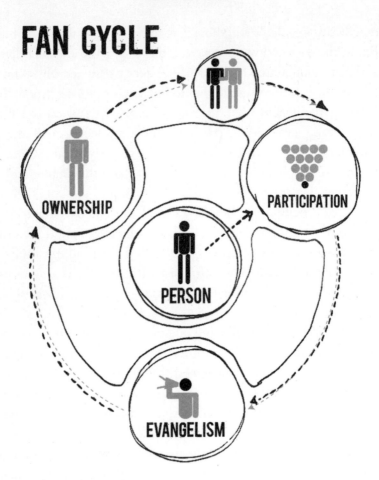

or cause. It is based in part on digital marketing expert and avid marketer David Armano's people graphic, and partly on *Citizen Marketers* authors Jackie Huba and Ben McConnell's loyalty ladder model. It is a guide for developing tools for online and off-line conversations and for measuring those tools' success. As we start to engage the customers, employees, and others who make up a fan community we're developing, the fan cycle allows us to index behavior, engagement, and tools in a uniquely actionable way and create a fertile ground for meaningful interaction.

Participation

The seeds of participation are planted with a simple introduction. You have to get to know someone before you want to go to their party. The same is true with an organization or cause. So the first step is to allow the fans you already have—neighbors, employees, external advocates—to make a personal introduction. Your fans will be the first ambassadors of your brand. Introduce yourself to them and then empower them to make introductions—information, recommendations, and invitations—for you.

When an effective introduction takes root, the relationship should sprout the early buds of participation. Whether in person or on the Web, participation is about the experience. Once someone has made the decision to interact, is that interaction remarkable? Is it worth telling others about? Is it engaging enough to turn a casual user into a fan?

The most mature phase of participation is adoption. This is still a passive stage, on the cusp of blossoming into evangelism, and it's where your new acquaintances have decided they have something in common with you, something they like. Still, their involvement is more personal and passive, enjoying and embodying the relationship but not necessarily proactively telling others about it.

Evangelism

Evangelical fans should be treated like rock stars, since these extroverted loyalists bring more and more people to meet you. They are the ones who spread the love and turn a brand or cause into a thriving movement. And their involvement doesn't just go out; it returns back to you. Evangelists won't just bring people to the party; they'll also tell you what food you should serve and what music to play. And it's up to you to listen.

Evangelism centers on the idea that the thing you had in common comes to life as a well-defined cause, and at its most profound, a well-defined cause can change the world. It can motivate employees and neighbors and leaders alike to work toward a shared, world-changing objective, whatever that happens to be.

While the Internet has enabled fans to be more active, it has created a sort of cheap evangelism. By "cheap," we mean less physically involved. Talk has become cheaper than when you had to write a letter, make a phone call, or hold a meeting. Online communities and web sites are wonderful tools that permit fans, participants, and even passive customers to engage in conversations. College football teams have active, user-created social message boards that bring old fans, new fans, lurkers, students, and parents together into a melting pot of conversations. But this anonymous communication can come with a price: a lack of accountability. And because of this cheaper communication, fans are so busy talking to each other that they often forget the real power of word of mouth: face-to-face social currency.

As you gather and mobilize your evangelists, let them help you find the hubs of passion that already exist. It's important to realize when to create your own party and when to go where the party is already jumping. Sometimes you have the enormous gift of built-in centers of community excitement and conversations happening off-line, which are key building blocks for a movement. Web sites become a valuable online resource to augment and facilitate these off-line connections.

Ownership

Great brands and organizations are co-owned by the fans who blog, moderate, recommend, and protect. The key is to bestow on fans the ability to participate in the message. The more they are encouraged to lead and develop their own material, the more they will believe that the community and the experience belong to them. With your guidance, they become the keepers, helping you sustain the evangelist garden you have planted through the course of this cycle.

Moving from evangelism to ownership requires one big thing: sacrifice. True ownership calls for loyalty and the willingness of someone—a customer, an employee, a friend—to make an investment or personal sacrifice and accept shared responsibility for an organization's continued triumph. Whether it's taking the time to put up flyers or write a letter, spending the money to create their own swag, or any number of other activities, it's the real investment of personal time and resources in support of something they believe in.

We're not going to suggest that everyone use our examples for themselves and their businesses. One thing we've learned from our work with teenagers is that everyone has a voice, but they use it in many different ways. Talking with a company, athletic department, or organization about things they could improve about the fan experience is simply another way to take ownership versus just evangelizing.

The next time you've got a story to tell, post it on a community forum by all means, but also take some action. Tell somebody if it's appropriate; if it's a conversation about football, bring them to a game. They will thank you.

EMPOWER PEOPLE WITH KNOWLEDGE? WHAT ABOUT KEEPING YOUR SECRETS?

Yes, we live in an age when people encourage transparency. Open and honest conversations. Putting it all out there.

But let's reiterate the point we made at the chapter's beginning: Secrets are still as important as ever. When you have a secret—like the speakeasy restaurants that were featured in *GOOD* magazine—people are drawn to you. They want some of that. It's mystery. It's intrigue. Secret sauces. Secret recipes. Secret codes. Secret treasure, even. People want to know and be let in.

But you don't have to share all your secrets. Keep some for yourself. It's an important part of your identity. The things you hold in are just as important as the things you share. However, knowing what to share and what not to share makes the difference.

Now, we're not saying that your secrets have to be those deep, dark matters that you're trying to hide. We're talking about those secret things that make you tick. The things that others are always trying to figure out. You know, the *really* good stuff.

Movements Have Shared Ownership

> *"Every single day of my life I say the word Fiskateer to someone. Every single day."*

Laura – Fiskateer #1943

Which do you think is more powerful and authentic: you telling someone about your brand every single day, or one of your fans telling someone about your brand every single day? If you chose the latter, you're right. But to do that, you have to share ownership.

We're often asked what it means for company leaders to give up ownership—and why they have to do so. But that's the only way your movement will grow, because you can't own a movement. Nobody can. It belongs to everybody. However, when you bring those kindred spirits into the fold and let them know that you are really and truly all in this together, then a light switch turns on. People feel empowered to take the ball and run with it without any fear or trepidation. That's freedom, and a key to success as well. Justine Foo has another way to put it: "A community becomes a community when it behaves like a community. You need . . . cooperation to happen. You need . . . your customers . . . to feel ownership of that experience, instead of just communicating at them."

"A community becomes a community, when it behaves like a community."

Justine Foo – PhD of Complex Systems
and the Brain Sciences

So many companies are terrified to give up what they never had in the first place: control—especially control of the message. It honestly baffles the mind. They worry, "What if someone says something bad about us?" Great! It's an opportunity to learn, engage, and improve your organization. Cocreation is the next step. It's either that or your customers creating content without you. Which would you prefer?

Consider this: The best way to gain more control of what people are saying about you is to give control away. It's true. Because now at least you can participate in that conversation and engage in the shared ownership that has to be baked into the very foundation of any movement. It's critical, and it's the only way that your fans will pick up the banner of your company and march forward. Remember: You're not the leader.

HAVE THE COURAGE TO GIVE UP OWNERSHIP

Courage starts with the willingness to put quality over quantity, have real conversations with people, and let them know what an organization is all about. But it doesn't stop there. Customers and employees become advocates when they can connect their passion to the company and shape its message into their own. It takes courage to allow your fans to be your company's voice—for better or worse—and let them co-own a company's success.

"It's okay to hear the bad things, because now you are hearing them and can fix them."

Jay Gillespie – Fiskars,
Vice President of Brand Marketing

And what about that "What if someone says something bad about us?" question? We'll let Jay Gillespie of Fiskars answer that one: "It's okay to hear the bad things, because now you can fix them." And that's as brilliant as it is simple. But it does take courage.

BECOME FANS OF YOUR FANS

Love is a circular transaction. By becoming fans of your fans, you kick off the process of returning the love. Yes, you heard us correctly; we believe that it's time for brands to become fans of their fans. Consider how much the praise and support and admiration you receive would be amplified if you, the brand, were to recognize those fans—and, in turn, to praise them. This also acknowledges that it's not about you, and that it never was. As you reinforce that fact with your fans and turn that spotlight on them, the more love you'll receive. See? It's cyclical, and cyclical equals sustainable. When this philosophy begins to take root, it won't be long until you'll be famous for the people who love you . . . for the way you love them.

Shared ownership must be an intrinsic part of the movement from the very beginning. It's a vital part of everything you've read so far, and everything you'll read in the rest of this book. Finding the passion conversation in others means that you're asking them what they think, which inherently makes them feel valued. And feeling valued is a direct conduit of them buying in and caring about what you're doing, since it's based on their direct input. It's those first conversations in which the seeds of shared ownership are planted.

Even the barrier of entry creates shared ownership, because down the road, you're putting those keys in the ambassadors' hands and letting them answer the door when someone rings the doorbell. And now they're the ones who are inviting whom they deem worthy to join the movement.

But one of the greatest things that shared ownership can do for your movement is protect you. If you're giving ownership in the movement over to your fans, then they are the ones who will come out of the woodwork when you need it the most. They will look out for you in a thousand different ways—and the people who are actually coming to your defense will surprise you most of all. You might expect it to be the loud and the proud who are already spreading the word about you on a regular basis, and while they'll be there for you, the wallflowers will be there as well. They might not be singing your praises to total strangers, but they'll be the ones who provide you support when you need it most. Shared ownership means that your fans' success is your success, and vice versa, in good times and bad.

SHARED OWNERSHIP STARTS AT THE VERY BEGINNING OF A MOVEMENT

Go back in time with us for a bit: In early spring 2001, South Carolina's government agencies for tobacco control, health, and prevention (DADOS and DHEC) were getting their feet wet in youth tobacco prevention. Thanks to the massive master settlement agreement that many states received, South Carolina was in the beginning stages of organizing a youth tobacco prevention program.

The job of gathering a ragtag patchwork of adults and teenagers to comprise the related efforts fell to DADOS. On one particular

Saturday, the collection of teens, adults, and government agency folks had a single mission: come up with a name for the South Carolina teen anti–tobacco use program. At the end of the day, the adults in charge were delighted with the new name that they had all but forced on the teens: LIFE. The adults left for home, happy with themselves, and the teens left thoroughly uninspired.

Two young women, sisters from Greenville, reached out to their adult advisor, Carol Reeves, a director for a local coalition, the minute they arrived home. Heather and Nikki expressed their frustration that the adults chose a name for the teenagers' program. Reeves took their sentiments to heart and voiced her concern with the other adults in charge. After many conversations, it was decided that the group would go through the exercise again. And this time, they asked us—since we had several employees volunteer for Reeves's coalition—to facilitate a work session to get consensus on a name and a plan for the fledgling youth program.

We jumped at the chance to do so, but only if it was just teenagers. In other words, no adults besides those from Brains on Fire would be in the room. Needless to say, that idea didn't sit well with the adults, but everyone finally agreed, and the meeting was planned.

You would think that getting the adults out of the room would let the kids get down to business, but that wasn't necessarily the case. A few of the teenagers even showed support for the name that had previously been chosen. We faced the conflict head on and got the teens engaged in a conversation to help us figure out the lay of the land.

The opportunity to build something new gave the majority of the teenagers something few had ever tasted: ownership. And watching this was not wasted on us. Seeing their eyes light up and witnessing their engagement would soon become a cornerstone of the movement.

We wish we could say we solved the name issue that very day, but fate had a different story planned. That very night after the session, those same two sisters who were the reason for calling the meeting stayed up all night, determined to put their thoughts into action. Those thoughts led to a passion-inspired message: rage against tobacco-related illnesses, rage against the tobacco industry's manipulation tactics, Rage against the Haze.

They fired off an e-mail to Carol Reeves and us. We remember reading that e-mail and sitting in stunned silence. It was perfect, but would our state's government agencies buy it?

A final work session had been planned, so the girls decided to wait and present their idea at that meeting. Reeves worked behind the scenes to get both government agencies to agree that whatever name the teens agreed on, the state had to back it. Talk about a leap of faith!

As the session was called to order, Heather and Nikki took their turn and presented their idea for the movement's name. I wish you could've seen the eyes of the adults as the name was revealed. It was like a verdict being read in a courtroom. As expected, the views in the room were split. So a vote was taken, and Rage against the Haze was born.

Looking back, it was simple: Allowing the teens—the ones on the movement's front lines daily—to name the program was empowering. It gave them a voice from the very beginning. And it instilled a sense of ownership at the ground level. This would be crucial over the coming years.

FISKATEERS COMING TO THE RESCUE

The Fiskateer movement was ignited in 2006, and from the first month of its existence, we have received remarkable stories of members coming to the rescue for the brand.

As we've already told you, Fiskars makes more than just orange-handled scissors. At the time the community began, Fiskars also made consumables—paper, stickers, and the like—that crafters use to scrapbook and decorate to their hearts content. These papers come in many different patterns, and some even have glitter and other ornamental elements on them as well.

One of the first reports we received from a Fiskateer in the general community told us about a routine visit she made to her local scrapbooking store to replenish her supplies. She noticed that the merchant had a large display of Fiskars papers near the front of the store by the windows. As she approached the trays that held the paper, she saw that the papers' edges were curling up. She alerted the store clerk, who said she was going to move them to the back of the store so they wouldn't be in the sunlight. Apparently, because of so much glue and other substances on the paper, the sunlight was causing it to curl. While a normal, every-day crafter who didn't feel a sense of ownership in the brand might have not given this another thought, an empowered member of a community—who believes that Fiskars's success is her success—felt compelled to take action. And since she had a direct pipeline into the company, she contacted a lead Fiskateer, who contacted Fiskars engineers—who then literally stopped the presses on the next run of that particular paper, saving Fiskars hundreds of thousands of dollars. That's ownership in action.

Another story of ownership involving the Fiskateers played out like this: There is a certain warning placed on all packaging that has a certain type of plastic in it in the state of California. It basically states that the plastic contained in the product has been linked to health concerns, and that some people, such as pregnant women, shouldn't handle the product. A statewide law requires that the warning be placed on all plastic products—regardless of whether the product has that particular plastic (which Fiskars products do not).

As the story goes, a woman purchased a Fiskars product, got it home, used it—then read the warning on the packaging and proceeded to flip out. And yes, she just happened to be pregnant. She posted on her blog how Fiskars was a terrible company to do such a thing, and that everybody should ban their products. She talked about writing her congressman and taking legal action against the company. She went on other crafting message boards and blogs to say the same thing in an attempt to express her views to as many people as possible.

As all public relations departments would do, Fiskars prepared a statement to clarify everything. But before they could release it to the press, many members of the Fiskateer community found the posts and responded. In fact, they came out of the woodwork, did a little bit of homework—and were able to post follow-up comments on those blogs and message boards that completely defused the situation. That, again, is shared ownership in action.

SHARED OWNERSHIP ALLOWS YOUR FANS TO PICK UP THE BANNER AND MARCH FORWARD

When Rage against the Haze was ignited, we saw the writing on the wall when it came to budget. Whereas other states tucked their tobacco prevention monies into safe places where they could only be used for what they were intended, South Carolina was a different story. Rage didn't get all the money it was supposed to, and we knew that one day—and one day soon—the money would run out. So, as we have learned to do with every movement, we had to build it like it was going to last forever, and like we'd run out of money tomorrow. And it began with—you guessed it—shared ownership.

In 2003, two years after Rage was founded, the money did indeed dry up. Gone. None. Zip. We do what we can as a company, but we have to earn money to keep the doors open. So while we provided some support, our hands were tied. We gathered our teen leaders together and told them the situation. It wasn't that the South Carolina DHEC or Brains on Fire didn't support them; it was simply a matter of politics and lack of funding.

A lot of things could've happened at that moment, the most significant of which would have been that the teens looked around, felt satisfied with all the progress they had made in two years, and decided to disband the movement. Instead, they looked around, saw how much they had accomplished in the past two years, and decided to push forward. They weren't finished by a long shot. In fact, they were just getting started.

Right then and there, those teenagers took ownership of the movement. It was all theirs, and they ran with it. With very little money, very little support, and a helluva lot of determination, that group actually recruited more people into the movement that year than during the years when we had hundreds of thousands of dollars to spend.

BUT THEY'RE NOT USING OUR LOGO THE RIGHT WAY

Whose logo? *Your* logo? See, you're forgetting about shared ownership already; it's not your logo to lose. It doesn't belong to you, and you can't keep it sacred in some brand identity manual that sits on your shelf. So don't worry about people misusing the logo or using the wrong Pantone Matching System colors. It's your fans' logo. It's a badge of honor that they want to wear—so let them.

The IndieBound movement we ignited with the American Booksellers Association is a great example of this. Materials were created to kick off the program, based on "Eat. Sleep. Read." Soon, new content from the independent booksellers—which showed how they put their own spin on the messaging according to their own location and clientele—was showing up on sites like Flickr and YouTube. From banners that said "Snack. Nap. Read." and "Read. Think. Vote." to T-shirts that read "Peace. Love. Books."

Chief Marketing Officer Meg Smith of the ABA explains: "The ownership here has been translated to pride. And the words that the booksellers can use—the IndieBound words that they use to talk to their customers—underneath all that is this incredible sense of pride and excitement and enthusiasm and is a reinvigoration of what they do."

SHARED OWNERSHIP LETS "YOUR" MESSAGE BECOME "OUR" MESSAGE

Marketers try to build messages that will spread. But as we discussed earlier, a lot of companies want you to spread their message. When it comes to igniting a movement, it has to be our message.

Love146—an organization whose mission it is to end world-wide child-sex slavery—understood this concept from the beginning. They are more than happy to collaborate with their supporters and give them anything they need to go and tell the story of Love146. And the result is amazing.

The group's founder, Rob Morris, elaborates: "We have kids donating $10, $5. We have a kid that donated $3 that he collected by putting a jar on his desk at school for other kids to contribute. That kid is part of the abolitionist movement."

Do a quick Flickr, blog, or YouTube search, and you'll see how members of the abolitionist movement have made the Love146 story their own. It's shared ownership in action, but it's only because Rob and the rest of the staff at Love146 made a conscious decision to let it happen naturally. They are thrilled that people spread the message however they see fit. It doesn't matter how, as long as it matters to the individual.

WHAT SHARED OWNERSHIP MEANS FOR THE CREATIVE PROCESS

Having world-class designers in our midst, we're always curious to see how other creative people react to the idea of cocreating online and off-line tools for a word-of-mouth movement. So when we're out and about sharing our insights with others, the question ultimately arises: "How much of what you present gets actually implemented and produced?"

Creatives ask this question because most traditional shops are used to presenting all these great ideas and fantastic designs . . . only to have them get picked apart. For a number of reasons, really. But eventually, unless you have one of those clients who gets it, the concepts and accompanying designs get dumbed down, and what you end up producing looks like everything else out there. It's a constant struggle for a lot of shops.

So what's our response? That the overwhelming majority of our concepts and designs get implemented when we help ignite a word-of-mouth movement. Why? Because it's not coming from a creative team that works in a vacuum. It's being cocreated with the people who will actually use the stuff. (Note that we didn't say "crowd-sourced" here, okay?)

Subjectivity goes out the window when you cocreate, since everything is based on conversations with the customers. We get around the brand police by showing them not what we want, but what the customer wants. It's a cocreated movement, and it comes from courageous insight.

But you have to be ready to accept the truth. Because true participation in people's lives through courageous insight opens up opportunities for deeper connections.

Do you want your ideas and creative concepts to see the light of day? Then don't start with the customer "in mind," but actually *with* the customer. Anything that comes straight from their mouths is pretty damn hard to refute.

You Have Permission to Change the System

A while back, some of the Brains on Fire crew were in Sydney having lunch with Roger Dennis, an innovation strategist from

New Zealand. During this great conversation, Roger revealed something that he uses to encourage and activate advocates: a business card–size tool that has one simple message on it: "You have permission to change the system."

Wow.

Simply giving someone permission opens up a world of possibilities. They don't have to tread lightly or be afraid of repercussions. They don't have to fear the hierarchy; they have been given permission. When you give permission to employees, customers, and advocates, you are giving them a hall pass, a permit, official authorization. And the empowerment that comes along with that is amazing. As the fan cycle states, empowerment leads to evangelism. Evangelism leads to ownership. And ownership means that your fans' success is your success, and your success is your fans' success. That's what we call a win-win.

Such a simple yet powerful concept from Roger. The best part? It's not digital. It's not a Twitter strategy. It's not online social media. It's tangible. It fits in the palm of your hand. And it taps into one of the most basic components of human DNA: appealing to a person's sense of self-worth.

So grant permission—and watch what happens.

> "Tell Me, and I'll Forget. Show Me, and I May Not Remember. Involve Me, and I'll Understand."
> —Native American Proverb

In other words:

Tell me: When you do all the talking, it's only a monologue. You're mixed in with all the other brands out there blathering away. People forget you very easily.

Show me: Sometimes demos work. But again, demos are everywhere, from test-drives to free samples in the mail. Unless you make that demo experience *very* remarkable, you're not going to be remembered.

Involve me: People look at things differently when you involve them. Maybe it's because now they have a chance to invest themselves in something. Involvement equals ownership. And as we've seen, ownership is powerful stuff.

INTEREST LEVEL vs. MARKETING PLAN OF ACTION

So how can you involve customers in your company? Start small and then ask them—and then listen. There are *so* many companies out there right now that are asking and not listening. If you're doing it the right way, they'll give you ideas for involvement before long that you and your marketing department wouldn't think of in a million years.

Movements Have Powerful Identities

Fill in the blank: "I am a _____."

A mac? A PC? Card-carrying member of the NRA? Buddhist? Vegetarian? Skinhead? What would you fill in that bank with? Whatever it is, it's part of your identity. It's a label. It's something with which you identify and something you support. And, most important, it's a part of you.

As humans, we are fundamentally hardwired to desire to be a part of something bigger than ourselves, more important than we are alone. Because we all want to be bigger than we are. Religion, sports teams—even brands. We're always on the lookout for things that we can incorporate into our personalities—because it creates a sense of belonging. And we all want to belong.

One of our favorite books is *The Element* by Sir Ken Robinson, PhD. Here is what he has to say on this subject: "Connecting with people who share the same passions affirms that you are not alone; that there are others like you and that, while many might not understand your passions, some do."

"We want to see ourselves in a bigger story than just our own lives."

Rob Morris – Love146,
President and Co-Founder

Powerful identities help draw kindred spirits to you and give them a badge of honor to wear. It allows you to recognize others in the movement, be able to share their stories, and bond with like-minded people. It's an extremely powerful tool, considering that we spend so much of our lives being identified by what people call us. Getting a chance to say, "This is who I am in spite of what everybody thinks" in an authentic way can be a really exciting moment for someone. Joining a movement is a chance to take control of your identity rather than falling victim to someone else's labeling.

IDENTITY VERSUS BRAND

Our roots as a company are in what a lot of marketing people would call "branding." *Brand* is one those words that corporations love to hide behind. "It's not 'on brand'" is one of our least favorite terms on the planet. Ugh.

We've always used the word *identity*, because we feel that by finding your purpose in the world as a company, you unearth your soul. And when you put your very soul out there, you protect it, value it, and draw kindred spirits near. Your organization's identity is so much more personal than a brand.

So what makes someone adopt an identity? Design and identity are part of what helps us make sense of the world. It gives order to chaos. We are the collections of beliefs and values we are passionate about, and passionate people wear their beliefs on their sleeves.

Have you ever seen one of those cars that are literally covered with bumper stickers? It's like that vehicle is an open book, using those bumper stickers to shout out what the owner is proud to be: a lover of peace and goodwill, a fan of a team, a supporter of gay rights. You can sense the pride they have in these beliefs in the space of a short stoplight.

But what makes us long to tell and show (in the case of a visual identity) the world about our passions?

A friend of ours has a left arm that's completely covered with tattoos. Frankly, they are quite beautiful, and since each design clearly stands for something he is passionate about, some people are, well, pretty jealous. When someone asked him about them one day, he in turn asked them this simple question: "What are you willing to commit to?" Don't you love that? It's true—ink on skin is a pretty big commitment.

IT'S EASY TO PROMISE; IT'S HARD TO COMMIT

Look, it's great to have a brand promise. It can communicate your offering's characteristics, value, and what people can expect from you. But as we all know, promises are made to be broken. A promise is a set of words with your intention, but a commitment is action.

So, as our tattooed friend asked: What are you willing to commit to, *really* commit to? Wearing something on your skin—for everyone to see—that signifies who you are and what you believe in is a true commitment. And yes, it's hard—and scary—to commit. It means that you're going to be held accountable, and to a higher standard. You're placing your reputation squarely on that commitment.

Brand promises seem to change as often as tag lines do. But commitments should never change. So (as if you didn't know this was coming), what is your brand commitment?

That is why you can't fake or force a shared identity on your fans. It has to bubble up naturally. We often frustrate ourselves when we forget this and try to name a community in the same way that we name products or services. We need to focus on helping a community name itself, which is hard work. You must literally become a part of the community, listen hard, and let the members guide this part of the process.

Sometimes it just feels right. One of the original names someone tossed out for what are now the Fiskateers was "Scissor

Sisters." When Fiskateers was tossed out there, it just struck a nerve and stuck with everyone involved in the project—from the team at Brains on Fire, the Fiskars team, and the leaders of the movement.

SOLID IDENTITIES ARE POLARIZING

Like is not a Brains on Fire word.

Think about it: When you ask someone's opinion about something, will a response of "I liked it," or "It was okay," cause you to take action and stay at that hotel or dine at that restaurant? Probably not, because *like* is not a very convincing word. But *love* and *hate* are. And you should want people to *love* you or *hate* you, because it gives you something worth talking about. *Like* is a death trap. *Like* has no emotion. It's a word that people use when they could care less.

A great example of an identity that stirs up strong emotions is the state of Texas. After all, it's truly a unique culture unto itself. However, it didn't happen overnight. The Texas identity is one that's been developed over decades and an identity that the people truly own. That Texas pride is so strong because the people of the state own the identity and want to share it with others. There are the rallying cries of "Remember the Alamo" and "Don't Mess with Texas." And when a Texan meets another Texan outside the state, there's an automatic connection.

But let's face it, people either love the state or hate it. And isn't that the passion that a great identity should invoke?

SO BACK TO THE QUESTION AT HAND

I am a _____. It's up to you and your fans to fill in that blank, and not in a self-serving way. The movement must be a valid extension of who you are and why you exist. But now it's also an extension of who your fans are and why they exist. That's why shared ownership is so important.

The teens who worked on Rage against the Haze not only named the movement; they also coined a new term based on the training they received. We took a cue from Seth Godin and taught them what an idea virus is, and how it spreads from person to person. From that, they started calling themselves Viralmentalists™.

The Charleston Parks Conservancy Park Angels is very much an "I am a _____" name. They are not only protectors of the parks; they watch over the parks and are attached to them. They need the parks just like the parks need them. It was a natural fit for those who were willing to step up and take a vested interest in their public spaces. Executive Director of the Charleston Parks Conservancy (out of which the Park Angel movement grew) Jim Martin revealed this recent story: "One of our board members was sitting at a bar when he started having a conversation with the bartender. [He] said something about the Charleston Parks Conservancy, and she screams out, 'Hey, I'm a Park Angel!' A couple sitting at the bar turned to him and said, 'We're Park Angels, too!'" *That's* what it means to be a part of something bigger than yourself. It becomes part of your identity and a connection point to others, and it's how a movement takes root in people's lives.

"Hey, I'm a Park Angel," and the couple sitting at the bar turned to him and said, "We're Park Angels, too."

Jim Martin – Charleston Parks Conservancy, Executive Director

But possibly the most powerful identity we've had the good fortune to help discover was with Love146 (formerly Justice for Children International). Founder Rob Morris came to us with a problem: It seemed that a group of lawyers in Texas had trademarked the name "Justice for Children International," and Rob had until the end of the year to find a new name. After he told us his mission—to end child-sex slavery and trafficking throughout the world—we knew we had to help.

So Rob and some others on staff came to visit us, and when we all sat down, the first thing we asked him was why he was doing this. The story that followed that question—told below in Rob's words—absolutely floored us.

In 2002, a small group of friends and I traveled to Southeast Asia to see what was going on firsthand. While there, we visited a brothel with a couple of under-cover investigators and posed as customers. Having to [pretend to be] the very [people who] so repulsed [us] by far was one of the most disturbing experiences of our lives. We found ourselves standing in a room, looking through glass windows at little girls [in] red dresses being sold as commodities. [The children] were sitting there, watching cartoons on little television sets . . . and we were standing shoulder-to-shoulder with men who were purchasing . . . these young girls—by number. These girls had even the dignity of a name stripped from them.

One of the most disturbing things that night was the look in these children's eyes. There was nothing left there. There was no life left. They were just staring robotically—blankly—at these crackling little television sets. I remember one girl—my guess was that she was probably new to the brothel—[because] there was still a fight left in her eyes. She was the only one not looking at the television sets. She was staring out of the glass at us. I don't know her name. I'll never know her name.

But I'll never forget her number. Her number was 146. There was still a fight left in her eyes. There was still life left there.

As you can imagine, there wasn't a dry eye in the meeting that followed, and in telling his story, Rob gave us the new identity for the organization: Love146. They call themselves abolitionists because they are on a mission to abolish child-sex slavery and trafficking. And they consider it an honor to call one another abolitionists. It embodies a lot of things. Beliefs. Action. A mission.

But what if you're selling scissors or musical instruments? Love146 didn't make it about themselves; they made it about their mission. Your movement's identity should make your fans and ambassadors the guiding light. After all, it's about them, not you!

Naming Best Buy's musical instruments department movement required that we reframe the conversation. It wasn't about selling guitars and drums. We found that the employees truly had a passion of finding the music inside each of their customers—and then amplifying it. So "MI" doesn't only stand for Musical Instruments but also for the Music Inside. The 11? If you're a Spinal Tap fan, you know that 11 means going "one louder." Cranking it up past the norm. And so Mi11 was born.

NUMBERS DON'T MATTER, BUT NUMBERING DOES

Okay, so your fans join your movement. But how do they internalize that identity? Now that they have a sense of belonging, where do they belong in that movement? A lesson within a lesson we've learned is the power of a number.

It started with the teenagers in Rage against the Haze. When they joined, they were sent a package in the mail filled with various items (which we'll get into in the next chapter). The most important of these items was a set of dog tags with the engraved number that was assigned to them when they signed up. The numbers ranged from 1 into the thousands. We had no idea that it would be a uniting and powerful element of the program. Teens would compare their numbers when they met for the first time. It was a way to start a conversation and identify with others. And still, even nine years later, some of these teenagers, now adults, still wear their tags.

Because this idea worked so well, we used it for the Fiskateers, too. Each member receives a pair of special edition scissors that has FISKATEER #___ engraved on the blade. These crafters identify with that number; it becomes an extension of even their name. When they post videos on YouTube or even comment on blogs and message boards, they sign off with their name and their Fiskateer number. It's amazing. And no matter if they are Fiskateer number 9 or 4,376, they are proud of that number. It's a badge of honor.

The adoption of those numbers has propelled us to make it a staple of every movement we've help ignite because they reinforce that sense of belonging and identity. Not only are you a part of something bigger, but you have your own corner of it carved out for you that is yours and no one else's.

THE RALLYING CRY

Another element that's integral in building an identity for a movement is the idea of a manifesto. A rallying cry. An oath, even. Just as your company probably has a mission statement, movements need a set of words or a document around which people can rally. But they need to be very specific and speak directly to the cause.

The American Booksellers Association has the Declaration of IndieBound, which celebrates the spirit of local stores. Here's an excerpt:

> When in the course of human events it becomes necessary for individuals to denounce the corporate bands

which threaten to homogenize our cities and our souls, we must celebrate the powers that make us unique and declare the causes which compel us to remain independent.

While it's a bit tongue-in-cheek (it borrows language from the Declaration of Independence), independent booksellers use this set of words to remind themselves that while they are indeed each independent, they are all in this together. And that concept of "independently bound" not only began to permeate the independent bookseller community but also changed the way others began to think about their local booksellers.

> "People want to be a part of a success story."
>
> **Scott Monty – Ford Motor Company,**
> **Head of Social Media**

Meg Smith, chief marketing officer of the American Booksellers Association, gave us this anecdote: "Two weeks after Indiebound launched, I picked up a blog post from a person in St. Louis calling for an independent store to be built in downtown St. Louis [in which] he referred to it as an IndieBound store. IndieBound is definitely a movement. . . ."

We quickly learned when we were collecting insights with the Fiskateers that online gathering places for crafters tended to be filled with sarcastic remarks. They can be very intimidating places for new crafters or for those without a thick skin. So out of that learning was born the Fiskateer Oath, the basic principles of which state that we're all here to celebrate and share our love of crafting, and that we will build each other up—not tear each other down—no matter what anyone's skill level, belief system, or background is.

It's been a cornerstone of the community from the beginning, and one of the reasons thousands of crafters have been attracted to it: It's a place of positive energy. And when a fellow Fiskateer crosses that line, others quickly remind the community of the oath they took. Not only is it a litmus test to gain entry to the community; it's a way for them to self-police.

Mi11 has a creed that new members take: to "accept the duties that come with being a member"; to "promise to encourage others I meet along my journey and pass on the techniques, knowledge and passion that have been shared with me." It goes on to say that "I am here because I choose to be here and reserve the right to express my views to Best Buy and the Mi11 community in an honest, respectful manner at all times."

Each manifesto goes hand in hand with the identity that is wrapped around the movement, so it's authentic and speaks to the individual's higher calling. It's a guiding light, something the first or newest member can reference and reflect on and internalize repeatedly. It might just be a set of words to an outsider, but then again, it wasn't written for an outsider. It was written for the true believers.

IDENTITY AFFECTS EVERYTHING

Before you can think about the other elements in your movement—and get yourself all tool- and tactic-ized to death—remember that it has to be rooted in you: your tone of voice, attitude, language, and authentic nature. We hate to use Apple as an example (because everybody uses them as an example for everything), but the company that almost everyone strives to be like has just about no presence in social media. Why? Because they are being true to who they are.

If you're struggling with your identity, then you're probably struggling with everything else. However, once you really know who you are and why you exist, everything else becomes clear as day: How you should engage people. What tools you should use. How you should reframe the conversation. What conversations you should even be participating in.

Everything starts with identity. And if you're reading this and feeling something in the pit of your stomach, then maybe it's time to do something about it instead of starting that Facebook Fan Page for your company.

DON'T DENY YOUR DNA

We've found in the identity development business that a lot of potential clients want to "change" something about themselves. They want to reinvent or rebirth—breathe new life, even. And though that's all well and good, finding out what they can *become* is almost always directly tied to who they *are*.

That applies even if they have a tired, old company; even if they don't care about culture right now; or even if a change in leadership wants to make its mark on the company. You can't deny your DNA, because that is what holds the keys. It's going back and learning the stories of why and who and how this organization was formed. It's uncovering the original stories and reigniting that passion, entrepreneurship, and excitement of those start-up days. Because those stories are what people are going to care about, and pass along to others.

Never try to be who you aren't. That goes for a lot of things (even social media). If it doesn't feel true to you, then don't do it. You can't deny who you are and what you stand for; anyway, why would you want to? We guarantee you that there's something in that DNA of your company that's a gold nugget of inspiration you can move forward with. And embracing that DNA is one of the smartest things your brand could ever do.

Remember: We are hardwired to want to be a part of something bigger than ourselves. But a part of what? And how do you know what that is unless it has an identity? Do you want to be a part of it, if it's an identity that you can relate to, that gets who you are and what you stand for? And that goes way beyond the logo. It's in the language and imagery, the tone of voice, and the way that identity is consistently presented over many, many touch points.

Each of us has a unique identity. And we're drawn to different things or, at least, drawn to things in different ways. When it comes to word-of-mouth movements, the movement's identity—what you're hoping your fans will be a part of—is crucial. It must be authentic, transparent, a powerful extension of the company or organization.

If not, you'll end up in "just another" land faster than you can say, "Hey, let's start a Twitter account."

SAME TRIBE

Soon after we starting working with the organization that would later become Love146, we received this e-mail:

> We have a term we use often around JFCI [that] expresses one of our values well. When we meet someone or a group of people who just seem to "get it" or are very like-minded, we say "Same Tribe." For example . . . when we left Brains on Fire this past Tuesday, we got into our car, looked at each other, smiled and said "same tribe." All that to say . . . we like you.

What a great set of words. If a company's true personality shines through in every single thing they do—the people who work there, the work they do, the way they answer the phones, and even their very outlook on life—then they will attract like-minded people, and like-minded clients and vendors. It's amazing to watch it happen with big and small companies alike. It's a kinsmanship that creates loyal advocates. And given the right tools, loyal advocates help with the word of mouth. It's all about finding those in your tribe and speaking to them.

Same tribe. Look for them. And hang on to them, no matter what.

YOUR IDENTITY ISN'T THE IDENTITY OF YOUR COMPETITION

Your competition isn't those other guys in your industry. Your competition is life.

There is so much marketing-speak out there about how "we can differentiate you from your competitors" because "yours is such a crowded industry with so many noisy messages." And you know what the companies do that preach this? They just make that market more crowded and even noisier. What a bunch of crap.

What happened to finding a company's soul? What happened to compelling storytelling? What happened to mystery?

People are constantly telling us that they "want to be the Google of X." Sure, I understand what they're saying, but shoot higher. A section in one of Seth Godin's books describes a huge banner in the Web offices of Wal-Mart that reads, "You Can't Out-Amazon Amazon." Continuing on with that theme: Don't try to out-Google or out-Amazon or out-Nike your competition. Instead, find the spirit of what makes you who you are, and let your identity reflect it transparently—all the way to the core. That's where the ArborWears (look them up: www.arborwear.com) of the world come from. Do you think they try to out-Carhartt Carhartt? No. And Carhartt is petrified of them.

Now it's your turn.

LESSON #8

Movements Live Both Online and Off-Line

Listen closely to what we're about to say: 90 percent of word-of-mouth interactions happen off-line. Yes, you read that right. Nine. Zero. Percent. The good folks at the Keller Fay Group have done the homework, and it's no joke.

Look, social media is great. The Internet allows ideas to travel at the speed of light, and it connects us to both information and other like-minded people. But as great as all the Twitters and Facebooks and MySpaces and blogs and message boards and digital doodads are, they will never, ever replace the power of shaking someone's hand, looking them in the eye, getting kindred spirits in the room (or better yet, at your brand's Mecca), and laughing together, getting a drink, sitting at the dinner table—whatever. So many companies are getting caught up in the tactics of social media and word-of-mouth marketing; they jump right in and quickly get bogged down in the technical details. But we need to engage *people* first. After you talk with them and observe how they communicate and connect, the tools and tactics will be as plain as the nose on your face. No guessing. No need for redos. Nothing except forward momentum.

We've quoted Justine Foo—a PhD holder in complex systems and the brain sciences—several times in this book so far, but now we're going to unleash her. Justine has an amazing combination of extreme intellect and approachability and is more than likely one of the few neuroscientists actually involved in branding and igniting movements. She is part of the extended tribe at Brains on Fire and works with us on a regular basis. So what does she think about the Web 2.0 revolution?

> I've never been comfortable with social media. I think it's an oxymoron. What fundamentally makes us human? The big answer to that question is the social brain; and if you look at studies of what makes our brains different from animal brains, the biggest difference is in the front—the social part of the brain.

Justine leans forward in her chair and continues with great enthusiasm and a whirlwind of hand gestures:

> So what do we know about how the social brain works, and what [it] fundamentally [means] to have social cognition? Well, first and foremost . . . it's [a capacity] called the theory of mind—the ability to infer something about your motivations. It's my ability to put myself in your shoes and say, what was she thinking? What is she motivated about? That is at the heart of all social behavior; our [capability] to infer what somebody else is trying to do. When we talk about wanting to connect with kindred spirits, in some ways we are wired to connect with people we understand.

We asked Justine to clarify her point.

> We also use the theory of mind for [social behaviors like] mutual collaboration and cooperation. Recent brain studies show that mutual cooperation actually activates "pleasure centers"—for lack of a better word—in the brain. It's very rewarding to engage in cooperation and cooperative group behaviors. And from an evolutionary

point of view, [you can certainly see] why that might be the case. The brain's not ten years old. It didn't evolve with the online world. It's three and a half million years old; it evolved at a time when [humans functioned] tribally and needed some kind of cohesive bond as a way to confer survival advantage.

So as a result of that, you have to ask yourselves— now moving to the online/off-line question—what kinds of information do we use to infer a person's motivations, or [figure out] whether he or she might be a kindred spirit? . . . Most of that information is off-line information. It's nonverbal, intonation, or a look on a face. There is an area of the brain that some people argue is specialized for faces. Some people say, actually, it's not a face specifically; it's just an object that has a certain degree of complexity. But I think they're both probably right—because a face is such a salient symbol in the history of humanity that there appears to be a group of cells that we know respond more to faces.

And then she hits us with it: "So what do you lose when you limit something to an online social media campaign? Think about it. Can you really build community or ignite a movement when it only exists online without real people to people interactions? Don't even try."

A HISTORY LESSON ABOUT SOCIAL MEDIA

A newer movement that we're igniting as we write this book is for Colonial Williamsburg, the birthplace of the United States of America. While gathering insight for the movement's foundation, we heard this great nugget (and reminder) from Director of Brand Strategy and Marketing Communications Sally McConnell: "The American Revolution was ignited by word of mouth; and it wasn't on the Internet. It was people riding up and down the East coast. [That] was their 'social media.' America's Storytown—this movement—will become a part of the new history."

Are you currently focusing all of your efforts on your online strategy? We get it; it's important. But we can't stress enough that your online has to drive your off-line, and your off-line has to drive your online. You want online to be powerful? Then use it as a tool that enables face-to-face. Remember, 90 percent of word of mouth happens *off-line*.

You'll certainly have bragging rights if you have 100,000 followers or friends or fans, but if it doesn't drive off-line, then what is it really good for? Integration is the key, and if you can't see the difference between the two, then you're blind. Which group do you think has the more powerful stories? Which group do you think has stronger emotional connections? It's one thing to sit at a desk and type and engage in a kind of passive participation. But to get up from behind the computer screen, walk out of your house, and become a part of something—to literally participate shoulder-to-shoulder—that's powerful.

So, yes, online is important. But off-line—that's where the real stories are created. It's where they live and breathe, because that's where we live and breathe. Know it; believe it; live it.

REAL PEOPLE + REAL COMMUNITIES = COMMONALITY

In the April 2009 issue of *Fast Company* magazine, writer Ellen McGirt interviewed Chris Hughes, who is not only one of the founders of Facebook but also the whiz behind the digital dominance that ultimately put President Obama in office. She writes:

> [Hughes] can't help but obsess about making technology less obsessive and simpler for everyone to use. He has

started to Twitter, albeit reluctantly. He worries about how over-connected people are, even himself: "I keep an eye on it." He thinks that Web 2.0 underemphasizes the real world and that businesses trying to tap the technology often miss the main point. His philosophy, he says, is unchanged from his first involvement with Facebook: "It doesn't matter if it's a company or a campaign; you build around commonality. If it's real people and real communities, then it's valuable. Otherwise it's just playing around online."

Chris Hughes is our new best friend. The beauty is that he created something that allowed people to meet online but then forced them to make the *real* connections off-line, all around a specific common *cause*. We can't emphasize enough that the real meat of any relationship is technology-free. You don't need it when you're sitting across the table from someone or hosting a dinner party at your house.

We live in a time when everyone is trying to figure out what to do next, and some individuals out there are pushing technology so hard that companies are jumping in without a plan just to have a presence online and "be connected." But connected to what, exactly? Most of the time that definition of connection is very superficial. It's just another way to try to get people to talk about that brand, all the while pushing out messages that are laced with "me, me, me." There's a lot of playing around online these days. And a lot of connecting, albeit in a shallow way, with people you have nothing in common with. It's overconnection for the sake of numbers. Remember the old statistic that states that we're hit with more than 3,000 ad messages per day? We wonder what that number is now, considering that so many brands are in our social networks these days. And while some of them are doing it the right way, that percentage is still very small.

Remember: A common bond is a common bond. And if you can find it—and enter into those conversations is an unassuming, transparent way—your fans will organize and put you into the proverbial White House. Just don't forget who got you there in the first place.

DEEPENING RELATIONSHIPS HAVE TO BE ACCOMPLISHED ONLINE AND OFF

As if we didn't talk about it enough already, here's even more proof from an article that comes from the British Science Association's British Festival of Science: Social networking sites don't deepen friendships. The gist is:

> "Although the numbers of friends people have on these sites can be massive, the actual number of close friends is approximately the same in the face to face real world," said Will Reader at Sheffield Hallam University.

In other words, connecting online is great. But all you're doing is forming acquaintances. People you might recognize and say "hey" to. (Or even more realistically, those people you ask, "How are you?" and they reply, "Fine.") But they're not people with whom you have deep conversations.

Now let us apply this notion to the brands that are getting involved in online social networking sites. For a lot of them, it's a numbers game. "How many people can we get to be fans on our Facebook page or friends on our MySpace page or follow us on Twitter?" But these are mere acquaintances with the hope of maybe somehow driving transactions. There's no intent for a real, deep relationship.

The article goes on to state that "90% of contacts that the subjects regarded as close friends were people they had met face to face." That's nine-oh percent. Wow. So now you may say, "But we as a brand simply can't afford to just throw parties for our customers all the time all over the place." And to you, we respond, you don't have to. You, as a brand, can become an enabler. As we've stated before, you don't throw a party and hope people will show up. You go to where the party is happening—off-line. And not like a bull in a china shop, either. Go hat in hand and humbly.

Now we're not saying in any way that you shouldn't develop an online strategy. But what you should do is figure out how that online strategy can drive *off*-line conversations, *off*-line gatherings, and *off*-line relationships with employees and fans. Online fundamentally needs to support *off*-line, and the other way around. They work together. And any company that tells you to put all your eggs in the online basket will get you plenty of acquaintances but not many meaningful relationships.

Back to the article mentioned before:

> "What social network sites can do is decrease the cost of maintaining and forming these social networks because we can post information to multiple people," [Reader] said.

> But to develop a real friendship we need to see that the other person is trustworthy. "We invest time and effort in them in the hope that sometime they will help us out. It is a kind of reciprocal relationship," said Dr Reader. "What we need is to be absolutely sure that a person is really going to invest in us, is really going to be there for us when we need them . . . . It's very easy to be deceptive on the internet."

There you go. A real relationship is about personal investment and sacrifice; this shouldn't come as a surprise to anyone. We ask you, the individual: How many companies that you have a relationship with will really be there for you when you need them? And to the brands, we ask: How many fans do you have that will do the same?

IT'S NOT ONLINE VERSUS OFF-LINE; IT'S ONLINE *WITH* OFF-LINE

Okay, so we've made the case that online has to support off-line, and vice versa. But how do you do that? Great question. So we'll dig further into the case studies and show you.

When we first incited the Fiskateer movement, we didn't tell members that after they joined through the web site, they'd be getting an actual physical package in their mailbox a couple of weeks later. Nothing like a little surprise and delight to get people talking, right? So when those boxes showed up and those Fiskateers opened them, they saw several things. We mentioned the scissors with the custom-colored handles and the Fiskateer number engraved on the blade in the last chapter; while this was a gift, it also served a specific purpose.

Crafters often get together in groups at what they call "crops," which are basically modern-day quilting bees. They bring in all their tools in suitcases and rolling caddies and spread out their work and scrapbook for hours on end. They share tools and tips, so a lot of conversations take place about their passion. When a Fiskateer shows up at a crop, she unpacks her tools and starts using her special scissors. Inevitably, someone asks, "Hey, I've never seen scissors like that before. Where did you get those?" And a conversation about Fiskars and the Fiskateers ensues.

We also included coasters with messages on them in that welcome kit and for use at crops. Again, crafters put down coasters at these crops so their beverages don't leave wet rings that could damage their table, work, and papers. We simply turned a functional item they already used into an invitation; when Fiskateers met someone they thought would be a great addition to the movement, they could give the person a coaster and suggest checking out the web site. That's a great example of off-line driving online.

Also in the welcome kit is a booklet that contains several things: a page that welcomes newcomers to the movement, information on what you can expect from Fiskars (sneak peeks to new products, invitations to Fiskateer-only events, etc.), a page on what we expect from you (honest feedback, participation and engagement, your time), and, of course, the page that has the Fiskateer Oath.

One of the stories we like to tell is about our designers at Brains on Fire spending a lot of time creating the beautiful "Now What?" booklet. They were very proud of their handiwork, and when people began to receive their welcome kits in the mail, we watched with anticipation for their reactions. They loved the books—especially the content—but as crafters, they couldn't resist the urge to reuse the paper. So they began to tear apart the books and utilize them for some of their other projects. The designers were surprised, but it's something we could have never seen coming. Now we cocreate materials with the community in the first place. Lesson learned.

Today you can find www.Fiskatools.com, a site where members can download and personalize their own Fiskateer business cards and coasters, put blinkies on their web sites, and share the oath with others. It's online and off, working hand-in-hand.

Another off-line element that trumps online technology is face-to-face events. During the first year of the Fiskateers' existence, we identified 50 of the most active and passionate members, and Fiskars gave them an all-expense-paid trip to San Antonio, Texas. They dubbed themselves the "Nifty Fifty." This gathering was conceived for a few reasons, the main one being to strengthen the core of the Fiskateer movement by letting people bond in person. These relationships had been cultivated online for months, and now Fiskars had the chance to solidify these potentially lifelong friendships. And so that's what we did.

The weekend was full of Riverwalk tours and visits to the Alamo, but we also took the Nifty Fifty though the same curriculum we took the leads through. There was plenty of time for impromptu crops, and we brought in crafting celebrities to lead classes. We also taught these 50 crafters how to teach certified demonstrator classes and charged them with going back to their homes and certifying 20 others each, thereby making sure we had 1,000 people around the country who were certified to teach classes on how to use Fiskars tools. Why? Because before this event, companies like Wal-Mart would call Fiskars and say they needed someone to come out and teach a class in, say, Dallas. Fiskars would have to scramble to find someone and often couldn't find anyone to send. But now Fiskars can give a Wal-Mart store in a given location a list of names and contact information. Wal-Mart will pay that individual to come teach a class, Fiskars will get more exposure, Fiskateers will get to teach the hobby they love to others, and we will watch that store's sales increase for the following 10 days. That's what they call a win-win situation.

The next year, we had five "Fiska-frenzies" all over the country. This time, we opened the event to all Fiskateers and required that they pay their own travel, but Fiskars covered the costs of the day. Each location was themed, and Fiskateers drove hundreds of miles to attend. We ended up getting 12 percent of the community to engage off-line in this manner, and now Fiskateers initiate and organize their own events. We don't even hear about them until they send us the pictures or post the images and videos online. So yes, we had to prime the pump, but now it's self-sustaining and doesn't cost Fiskars a dime.

GO WHERE THE PARTY IS HAPPENING

A common saying around our halls is "Don't throw a party and expect people to show up. Instead, go to where the party is happening." Would you really want to leave your party to go to someone else's you don't really know all that well, and then as soon as you hit the door, all they talk about is themselves? "Come on in. Welcome to *my* party. We'll be discussing the following topics: (1) How great I am. (2) All the cool things I do for you. (3) More ways to tell me how great I am."

Yeah, we wouldn't want to go to that party, either.

A great example of this theory in action is our work with teen-agers and Rage against the Haze. Anyone who's worked with teenagers knows that it's hard work to try to organize an event and then hope against hope that people will actually show up for it. So why not go where the party is already taking place, somewhere teens are already gathered and open to conversations? Why not meet them on their turf, instead of hoping they will come to a strange place and open up to people they don't really know in this new environment? That just doesn't make any sense.

As you might guess, on any given autumn Friday night in South Carolina, entire towns empty out to go to local high school football games. That's really not much of an exaggeration. So obviously, since that's where the party was, that's where we went. Each Friday, our team of teens would show up at the biggest rivalry high school football game in the state. Sometimes they were in cities you've heard of before, like Charleston and Greenville, but many were in towns you've never heard of, like Star, Moncks Corner, and Camden. And while we did set up a booth, we'd also go out and talk to people. We'd get the cheerleaders involved, and they'd throw swag out into the crowd. We had a drumming challenge with the band. We'd interview the senior class president and football coaches. But there was no preaching about the dangers of tobacco. There were just conversations. Peer to peer. Using plain language and relating to one another.

High school student Quentin James played an integral role in the ignition of the Rage movement, and he went to work on the movement to elect President Obama as well. He was one of the team members who traveled around South Carolina to meet other teens where they were. He said, "With Rage, there was this constant stream of excitement every Friday night when we traveled to different games. Whether it was the high school events or the prom challenge, with every project we reinvented ourselves."

These are things that just don't happen online and provide a depth that can't be replicated when you're sitting behind a glass screen and a bunch of wires. For the Charleston Park Angels, it's getting your hands dirty in the parks while learning about the rich heritage of the plants. For Best Buy's Mi11, it's seeing local bands and meeting new musicians—not to mention making new musicians when you introduce them to a new guitar or drum set. For Colonial Williamsburg, it's immersing yourself in the place where America was born. You can't do that online, no matter how advanced the experience may be.

YES, ONLINE IS IMPORTANT

You will never hear us say that online engagement isn't important. Remember, the best strategy is to figure out how off-line and online can work together to become a powerful force to be reckoned with.

But . . .

Don't create a Facebook fan page because your competitor is doing it. Don't jump on the Twitter bandwagon just because it's the flavor of the month. Remember that thing called Second Life? Yeah. Good one.

" It's like the philandering girlfriend. Technology is not going to stay faithful to you."

Chris Sandoval – Member Experience Strategist
for a diversified financial services group serving
the Military community.

As our friend Chris, who is in experience design with a large financial services company that's geared toward the military and miliary families, reminds us, "It's not about technology; it's about people. I've worked in the tech field since the mid-nineties. The minute you fall in love with any given technology, it's outdated. It's like the philandering girlfriend. Technology is not going to stay faithful to you."

We love his phrasing because it rings so true, and it helps us look at things in a new light. Sure, you can trust in technology if you want and see where that gets you. But what you should trust in is that technology will always change. But the fundamental reasons people use it never do.

If you're sitting down to think about technology strategy first, you're going to have to go back to the drawing board in a few months. You'll constantly be playing catch-up. But if you invest in a strategy that engages your employees and customers first, then you'll be ahead of the game. It's the difference between blindly creating something *for* people, or intelligently and openly creating something *with* people. It's your choice.

So instead of going off into a corner and developing your iPhone application, why don't you ask your fans *how* they connect with one another first? Do your fans even have iPhones? Why not approach them and facilitate a conversation before you take action? We are so quick to *do* without answering the *why* of what we're doing.

A couple of years ago, when Twitter and Facebook were new on the scene, it was easy to become enamored with those shiny objects. However, instead of rushing into them, we actually had a novel idea: we *asked* the Fiskateer community what they thought about those social media tools. And they cringed. The overwhelming majority of them didn't go near either of those applications. Obviously, the time wasn't right. We couldn't build it and hope that they would come, when they were more than happy with the current Fiskateer site with all its bells and whistles (message boards, blog, galleries, chat rooms, etc.). So after listening to what the people wanted—or, in this case, didn't want—we put our efforts into making the current site even better.

Fast-forward three years. Twitter is really starting to take off, and we see more and more of the Fiskateer community dipping their toes in the Twitter water. So we engaged once again, but in a way that attempted to get people comfortable with the application, not force it on them. We noticed at the time that when a Fiskateer would find a great deal in a retail shop on Fiskars products, they would post what they called an "enabler alert" on the message boards to let others know of their find. Within minutes, we saw replies that said, "Oh, I'm going there at lunch!" and "Thanks for the tip." We knew right away that this was a valued service that ambassadors provided one another. They took pride in finding deals and sharing them with the community, and that got us thinking about how we could incorporate the two.

So we started a Twitter account called Fiskadeals. Keep in mind that even as we write this in early 2010, there still aren't a lot of Fiskateers tweeting. So instead of leaving it at that, we worked with a Web development company to devise an application that Fiskateers could put on their blogs as a direct Fiskadeals Twitter feed. When someone posted an enabler alert on the message board, it would get picked up by the Twitter feed and then blasted out to hundreds of blogs. Again, Fiskateers saw themselves as spreading valuable information. So while we did end up using Twitter, we had to do so in a way that could really benefit the community, instead of doing it just to do it.

The point is that you don't need to jump on the bandwagon when you integrate technology. We need to keep in mind that people are the killer app. Flesh and blood trump wire and glass every time. This is fundamental, and it will never change. So you can either roll with it or fight against it. One way will enlighten you, and the other will destroy you.

Lesson #9

Movements Make Advocates Feel Like Rock Stars

Wouldn't it be nice if Lexus found out that you were a huge fan and gave you a free car? Or if JetBlue gave you unlimited free airfare in return for your constant raving about them? Or if Whole Foods found out that you told all your friends about your grocery shopping experience and you got free groceries for life? Of course, that'd be great. But it's not exactly reality, and not a great business model, either.

When we tell you to treat your advocates like rock stars, we're not talking about champagne wishes and caviar dreams, or private jets and penthouse suites. Yes, those things are nice. But you're not going to have a movement if you try to reward people with free stuff through sweepstakes and contests. That's part of a campaign, and it won't make people feel appreciated. Just lucky.

A more effective approach is to reward people with recognition. And don't just shine a light on the overachievers; love the ones who hardly have any time to give to the movement but do so anyway. Listen to the haters as well as lovers. But don't listen from the shadows like some CIA operative who's undercover in a foreign country. Listen *actively*, like you're sitting across the table from your advocates, looking them in the eye, nodding your head, and taking notes. *Really* hear the words that come out of their mouths, and then engage. Again, it's not about giving people swag or money or any of those material things. When you make someone feel like a rock star, *you*, the brand, are becoming their fan. Remember that.

"We need to be given the outlet and, more importantly, appreciated for our efforts."

Angela – Fiskateer #009

Lead Fiskateer Angela Daniels (#009) summarized this idea beautifully: "Maybe some people are born advocates. We're just looking for something to advocate for; and to do that, we need to be given the outlet and, more importantly, appreciated for our efforts."

We hear about a lot of companies that want to create fans for their brand. However, it needs to be the other way around. Don't find people to lift you up; you lift them up first. Be famous for the people who love you, for the way you love them. As we've stated before: Love and recognition form a circular transaction. If you give it out, it'll always come back to you—in spades.

Here's a viewpoint from Ford's Scott Monty:

Having the support of your network, enthusiasts, [and] advocates—and nurturing those relationships—[will] ultimately build loyalty and trust over time. And that's much more than just building a fan base. It's really about exploring those relationships and ensuring that you're providing value to them every step of the way.

LIFTING UP YOUR CUSTOMERS

When we first started in this business, part of our mission was to lift others up. Don't worry, we're not going to get all religious on you (though you can travel down that path if you like).

Think about that set of words for a second: "lift others up." It's your job to find passionate people, hoist up their conversations, shine a light on their lives, raise the sails of what they care about, and connect them with companies that care to have a real relationship—one that transcends a Twitter feed.

When your goal is to lift someone up, you think about things differently. You are the one making the efforts, not them. You are providing the footholds, the rope, the initial push, whatever it takes. You're not trying to manipulate them or get them to do anything for you; instead, you are enabling them. You're celebrating them. You become the conduit. And that's a lot stronger than your social media campaign.

So think about things differently. Lift others up. Is it back-breaking work? You bet. Is it worth it? Every. Single. Minute.

Here's a great example that Fiskars's director of communications at the time, Suzanne Fanning, wrote to the Fiskateer community when the 5,000th Fiskateer joined:

> This is a day to celebrate! As of last night, we officially have 5000 Fiskateers. Everybody please welcome Fiskateer #5000—Sally from Silver Spring, MD!
>
> Well, Sally, you are kind of like the New Year's baby here. On behalf of Fiskars, I am authorized to send you to one of the Fiskafriendzies of your choice. All 4,999 of us want to know . . . will you be dipping candles in New England, becoming a crafting country star in Nashville, setting sail in California, sampling chocolate in Hershey or hitting the rails in Nevada?
>
> But I also want to take this chance to tell you how special ALL of you are to Fiskars. This movement has been unbelievable. You are all talented, creative, passionate, wonderful, caring supportive advocates for

us and for each other. This community has turned into more than we ever could have imagined.

Laura recently [wrote] a beautiful post entitled "Because of Fiskars," and I think this is an appropriate place to republish my comment back to you all.

Because of Fiskateers . . .

Fiskars has the most creative and innovative friends anyone could ask for. We cherish every opportunity to travel across the country and meet you face-to-face, because you teach us so much every single time; not just about products, but about passion, love, art and joy. We try new things every day to delight you, and we know that our friends are even true enough to tell us when we are wrong. But we also know that there is NOTHING like the shout of orange and green glory when the Fiskateers let us (and everyone else) know that we have done something right! Of all the beautiful "Fiska" words in the world, none is more important to us or warms our hearts more than "Fiskateer." Thank you from Fiskars!

DON'T YOU WANNA BE IN THE CLUB?

We've established that people naturally want to be part of a tribe and in on its secrets It makes them feel special, even important. There's a certain amount of pride that people take in the fact that they are walking around with knowledge that other people don't have. And that makes them want to talk about it. After all, first to know is first to tell, right?

You've hopefully seen throughout these pages that all the elements of a movement have to lock together, and that some of them even overlap. Making advocates feel like rock stars is one of those overlapping factors. And here's why, while you're building other elements of your movement, you're actually building this one as well.

Remember the theory behind a barrier of entry? A membership structure that invites and is elite is much more effective in creating a free movement that *everyone* can join. People who want to join the Fiskateers e-mail a lead, telling them about their passion for creating and crafting. The lead then gives them the secret site to register and asks general questions to make sure they are true crafters and not just looking for free stuff. The freebie seekers typically weed themselves out at the beginning of the process, anyway. But when you have to apply to be a part of something and are accepted, it's a nod from the brand that you're one of us. You're a kindred spirit. And we trust you.

Giving the movement a powerful identity also helps establish that rock star feeling. It's a great way to make membership more significant. As we discussed, for the Fiskateers, it was as simple as assigning an individual number ("I'm Fiskateer #2047"). It's a source of belonging and pride, but it also lets members know that they have a permanent place in the movement, that nobody else in the world will have that number—ever—except them. And the Fiskateers love their numbers. They sign e-mails and projects with them.

Another way to love your advocates is, yes, by giving them something. But not necessarily big-ticket items, just a form or recognition in something that nobody else can get except other members. Members of Rage receive their dog tags in a welcome kit. Fiskateers receive their special scissors. Park Angels receive wings. Colonial Williamsburg fans receive a replica of an old, historic key to the city. Brains on Fire even has an underground site (www.youareoneofus.com), where we send advocates to pick out their own special Brains on Fire gear. This concept also lends itself to a sense of community. Remember the LIVESTRONG yellow bracelets from the Lance Armstrong Foundation in support of cancer research? When you wore one and saw someone else wearing one—say, in an airport or a restaurant—you probably made eye contact and smiled. That person was a stranger to you before, but the commonality gave you a reason to have a conversation. It's a connection point, and that's what these small, cost-effective, exclusive gifts can bring to the movement. And along with that connection point comes a feeling of pride and ownership, which makes advocates feel like rock stars.

Consider the perspective of Chris Ivan, one of the original Viralmentalists for Rage against the Haze, on the importance of off-line tools for engagement: "I am still very happy and excited when I see my RAGE dog tag. Sometimes I use them as props when I go to an event; or just for fun times, I wear them and they can spark a conversation. There's a story behind everything, right?"

THE CENTER OF THE UNIVERSE EXPERIENCE

Where would you consider your own personal center of the universe to be? Is it the stadium where your favorite football team plays? Maybe it's where your fly-fishing rod was crafted, or even the plant where your car was made. We all have those places we'd like to visit to see where the magic really happens, where our favorite brands were conceived and grew. Maybe it's Nike HQ in Oregon or the flagship REI in Kent, Washington. How about where the original American Girl doll was sewn together? Each of these places is the center of the universe for someone, and while it may not be important to everyone, yours is important to *you*. And that's all that matters.

Allow us to tell you about one nondescript building in Madison, Wisconsin. It's gray and has a lot of cubicles. To you and me, it's not remarkable. But when we brought the four lead ambassadors for Fiskars there, they walked in the front door and *squealed*. It's Fiskars's North American headquarters, and for crafters, this is where the magic happens. Within those doors are next year's designs, the engineers who fashion the smallest details of what goes on the shelf, and essentially all the secrets that *every* hard-core crafter wants to know. And when you open those doors to your fans, you're creating a center of the universe experience.

Such experiences come in all shapes and sizes. Back in its heyday—from 1994 to 1999—Saturn's Tennessee plant held homecoming events to give Saturn owners a chance to visit the place where their baby was born. And came they did, by the tens of thousands (44,000 in 1999). They bonded and traded stories about the cars they loved.

Louisville-based whiskey company Makers Mark hosts an annual experience called "Redheads and Thoroughbreds" that coincides with the Kentucky Derby. In addition to parties that feature the dark liquor, there are tours of the distillery where you can dip bottles in the iconic red wax to seal the tops. There are special racing events just for Makers Mark ambassadors. And you better believe they bond over the drink that's bringing them together.

So is going to a car plant in Tennessee or traveling to Wisconsin to meet scissors designers remarkable to you? Probably not. But you'd be surprised at the things that thrill certain people. Sure, you might be concerned that your product or service isn't sexy, that it's not an iPod or a sports car or a drink that people order at a bar. You might worry that people aren't going to talk about it because it's not exactly what most folks would call cool.

Well, you're mistaken.

When you really engage and participate in your customers' lives, you can begin to understand what makes them tick. And what's even better is that you'll come to understand what they're passionate about. But you have to look at it from their perspective. It's not about how *they* fit into your marketing plan but rather about how *you* fit into their lives. It's about reframing the conversation, remember?

You'd be amazed at what people will willingly spend their time and effort on when they're passionate about something, no matter if it's scissors or musical instruments or books or tires. You just have to dig for what is relevant to them—not to you.

SWAG THAT EMPOWERS

In the very beginning of the Rage against the Haze movement, we created a lot of swag, which means that the teens had access to a lot of cool gear: T-shirts, messenger bags, stickers, you get the idea. But our limited budget allowed us to have only limited quantities of these items.

We never told the original leaders of the Rage movement that they had to be judicious about giving away swag, but the restricted quantities and the cool factor of the gear prompted the teens to value it highly. They didn't want just anyone to have the gear, only those who were dedicated to the anti–tobacco use movement. So when someone finally earned an item, a rock star moment was created. This occurred completely organically, which is the best way for it to happen.

THE CLOSEST THING TO BEING A ROCK STAR

Is being on stage. So do it. Put your customers on stage. Get your big old branded butt off the stage and away from the microphone. I know it's hard. We like to hold on to that mike for all it's worth and blast out our message in hopes that the crowds gather and chant our name. But at the bottom of your heart, you know that's really never going to happen.

So instead of fighting it, embrace it. Once you find those advocates and empower them with the tools they need, it's time to amplify their voice to the world. So be their roadie. Set up the stage just the way they like it. Put all the tools in place. Make it perfect for their appearance. And you know what? People who would never have wanted to see *you* on stage start to gather and listen to someone they can relate to. That person on stage now is "just like me," and that intrigues people. It lets them see themselves in that same position: holding the mike in front of thousands who are hanging on their every word and actually participating in the movement themselves.

RESPONSIBILITY = APPRECIATION = OWNERSHIP = ROCK STARS

Of course, you should treat the leaders of your movement like rock stars. But you should also treat volunteers—those hand-raisers in the community who dedicate their time, efforts, attention, and money to their passion—like rock stars. A great way to do that is to give them ownership through responsibility. Assign them tasks that you know they can handle.

For Rage against the Haze, it was asking members to weigh in on the gear and designs. As you read previously, because of their involvement, it wasn't just a T-shirt. It became something of value, something that they got to choose how to use, and ownership ensued.

We gave the Fiskateers opportunities to organize around sub-passions within the community. We noticed that when a new member joined and introduced herself on the message board, the same group of people would typically show up, welcome her into the community, and help her plug in. So why not help them organize and empower them? They were already raising their hands. We gave them a very small stipend of product that they could do with whatever they wanted.

Then we found out about a group that loved to do charity crops, so we helped organize and empower them as well. We found clusters dedicated to gardening, school crafts, Gen X, and more. We identified subgroups, talked with them, and asked how we could amplify their passions.

The point here is that it doesn't stop with just organizing a community. Your job isn't done when you turn on the web site. It isn't even completed when you gather kindred spirits and invite them into that community. In fact, if you're doing it right, your job is *never* really done. The next step to deepen the movement's roots is to find the hand-raisers, call them out by name (in a good way), recognize them, and then empower them to recognize others. Love is a circular transaction—remember? It just goes on and on and on as long as the empowerment goes on. And it's up to you to kick that cycle off.

THE LITTLE THINGS ARE BIG THINGS

We *should* say: The things that are little to you more than likely aren't that little to your fans. What you might consider unimportant and mundane—items that get lost in your day-to-day responsibilities—may mean a lot to one of your brand's advocates.

The simplest of these is the power of "thank you." When you thank fans, you're acknowledging their contribution and giving them attention. You're telling them you know they exist and that you appreciate all that they're doing—even though they don't have to do it.

For example, we at Brains on Fire have what we call the love bomb. Sometimes, out of the blue, one of us receives an e-mail from someone who stumbled across our web site or some of our work. These e-mails, filled with praise and congratulation, are always a bright spot in our day. So the recipient typically forwards the e-mail to the rest of the team, each of whom sends back a short note acknowledging the sender. Think about it: You take the time to write an e-mail to a company you like, and you receive in return 20 e-mails from people inside that company. It's such a small thing, but it makes such a big impact. Now we've turned that person who was curious about the company into a lifelong advocate, with very little effort.

TRUST

We've used this word throughout these pages. Trust must be a cornerstone of any movement. And that doesn't become any clearer than when you allow your advocates to say what they want, when they want, about what they want. Yes, it's scary. But when you trust them to do the right thing, you are empowering them. You are no longer the big bad brand controlling the conversation.

As fellow kindred spirit Tonya Polydoroff, a public relations specialist for a large international company, told us:

> We have a whole department for brand management and image awareness. Their job is to police the way that people talk about us and to make sure that our icon is used the proper way. We take really concerted efforts to make sure that those things are done. So [putting] something out there where people can comment completely freely—[that] we don't control— is definitely a scary thing for us.

The bigger the company, the scarier it seems to be to loosen that stranglehold on your own site when it comes to allowing people to say what they need to say. That's why trust empowers. And when you empower with something as important as trust, then people feel you have faith in them and want to do the right thing for you. The rock star cycle continues.

And of course, a great way to exercise trust in your advocates is to simply ask them what they think *before* you take action.

Not only does this instill a sense of ownership but also it lets those fans know that they're important. As Jay Gillespie from Fiskars told us, "We don't want to make a move without asking the Fiskateers." How many companies do you know that make such a concerted effort in putting their customers first?

"We don't want to make a move without asking the Fiskateers."

Jay Gillespie – Fiskars,
Vice President of Brand Marketing

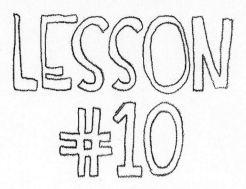

LESSON #10

Movements Get Results

Okay, cynics, we know what you're thinking: All this movement stuff is nice and squishy, but it doesn't matter one bit if it doesn't move the needle for my company or organization. And we couldn't agree more. That's the last point: A movement isn't a movement unless you move toward your goals in a significant way. That's why, in the very beginning—way back before Chapter 1—you need to set your goals and ask yourself what success looks like. And it's not *always* sales, although that's an important component of it.

To be honest, an increase in sales is a by-product of a movement. Sentiment, conversations about you, connecting like-minded people, and becoming a part of that relationship—now you're talking. The greatest thing you can hope to be is a conduit for a conversation, rather than the conversation itself.

Movements get results, like waking up your employees and opening their eyes to the fact that what they do matters. Like energizing your sales force. Like your fans stifling PR nightmares before you even have time to react. Like your fans creating their own marketing messages and gear, coming to your defense, helping you though the hard times, and cocreating new products. The list goes on and on, and you're going see results in ways you can't even imagine when you help ignite that movement.

"The American Revolution was ignited by word of mouth, and it wasn't on the Internet."

Sally McConnell – Colonial Williamsburg Foundation,
Director of Brand Strategy and Marketing Communications

CLOSENESS TO CUSTOMERS

There's a lot of talk about the return on investment of word-of-mouth marketing and social media lately. Maybe it's because we're all trying to find meaningful ways to justify effort and spending in the work we do in the world. In thinking about that, we ran across this phrase from Hermann Simon, author of *Hidden Champions of the 21st Century,* who is considered to be the Jim Collins (author of *Good to Great*) of the world of privately held midmarket companies: "closeness to customer."

It seems that of the hidden champions Simon has studied, 88.7 percent have the following characteristic in common: five times as many employees (25–50 percent) have regular customer contact. Compare this with larger companies that typically have only 5 to 10 percent of their employees making regular customer contact.

Think about that. Simon's hidden champions are number one or two in world market share, have less than $1 billion in revenues, and have low visibility and public awareness. An interesting—and, some might argue, odd—bunch for those of us involved in social media to learn from, for sure.

So what is the value of customer closeness? According to Simon, staying close to your most demanding customers compels performance and innovation. Strategies become driven by value, not price, so these companies can charge 10 percent to 15 percent more for their products or services. And we would bet money that employees are more engaged if they are closer to customers. It's always a signal of corporate health and profitability, in our opinion.

We have seen this at work firsthand in the movements we have cocreated with our clients. Being on a first-name basis with a larger group of your customers significantly changes the game. They are no longer your target audience; they are people, with fascinating lives. You find common passion and interests with someone you know more intimately.

So ask yourself this: How close is your *company* to your *customers?* What percentage of your employees have regular customer contact and conversation?

RESULTS, RETURN ON INVESTMENT, THE BOTTOM LINE

Advertising will not sell a bad product; it'll just make more people aware that it's a bad product. And igniting a movement will not sell a bad product either. Every marketer needs to start by making a better product. There are lots of ways to do that. One is to have a little internal team of expert that goes off and tries to make things better. But really, a more effective approach is to involve the people who are actually using the product.

One of our favorite lessons comes from Fiskars Vice President of Brand Jay Gillespie: "Today, we are constantly engaging the actual people that use our products. They are absolutely fueling better products." Read that again. Fiskars doesn't want to make a move without asking their customers first. And that's the way it should be.

"Today we are constantly engaging the actual people that use our products. They are absolutely fueling better products."

Jay Gillespie – Fiskars,
Vice President of Brand Marketing

The great companies of the world have understood this all along, on some gut level at least. Apple, Patagonia, USAA, Southwest Airlines—name a great company, and we'll bet you money that they don't just know their customers as well as they know a best friend; they hire their customers, too.

The world is more challenging and competitive than ever before. Innovation is not just a nice and lofty goal; it's something your customers demand.

After all, how do you measure the success of something that would never have happened? How do you measure the value of a 35 percent response rate on a 72-question survey about new products?

TYING IT ALL TOGETHER

Setting goals is paramount for a movement. After all, you have to move toward something, right? So just for the sake of closing the loop on the case studies we've discussed throughout the book, here are some of the results.

Everyone is talking about social media in terms of numbers of Facebook friends and Twitter followers. Everyone seems in search of bodies. But what about defining success in terms of engagement? Jay Gillespie has this to say about the numbers game: "For me, it's not about the numbers; it's about growing deeper relationships."

So how do you measure the power of engagement? Since the world of business has changed so dramatically in the last decade, we have to ask the question: Has the definition of success changed? Yes. Because you can't make a difference if you cease to exist. The bottom line is the bottom line.

Meg Smith from the American Booksellers Association puts it nicely: "If it wasn't for the igniting of the IndieBound movement, there would be less books being sold in independent bookstores; and part of that is because the booksellers themselves would have less enthusiasm about what they do."

The results for Love146 don't stop with doubling the amount of money they've raised to end child-sex slavery since they changed their name and identity. It's also about connecting with an entire new audience on a deeper level. Founder Rob Morris says it all with this:

> You know, when I've been traveling [which I do a lot], a classic conversation . . . takes place with the person sitting next to you on an airplane. They're, you know, "So are you going to Thailand on business or pleasure?"
>
> And I reply, "I'm going on business."
>
> "Well, you know, what do you do?"
>
> "I'm a part of a human rights agency called Justice for Children International."
>
> [And that was usually where the conversation ended] when our name was Justice for Children. It was just sort of like, "Oh, that's great." [But renaming it] Love146 [has] produced another question 100 percent of the time; which was "Love146, what is that?" And thus, a story is immediately told. And I've had people in tears on airplanes traveling because of the story.

Success for the Charleston Parks Conservancy (the Park Angels movement) comes in a different package as well. According to the Executive Director Jim Martin, it's a city that now spends time working in its public spaces. "After starting the Park Angels movement in January 2008, we're now working in over 10 percent of our . . . over-120 parks." And that number continues to grow. So the Charleston Parks Conservancy went from being a foundation that hosts fund-raisers to a place where citizens of Charleston can learn about the rich horticulture of their city's history by participating in the nurturing of their public spaces. How does one measure that?

Rage against the Haze accomplished amazing success. The 2006 South Carolina Youth Tobacco Survey found that South Carolina had a smoking rate drop of 16.9 percent, one of the highest in the nation. That's without any kind of mass media or tax increases on cigarettes. According to the American Lung Association, this is an unprecedented drop, and this is the state with the cheapest cigarette prices in the nation. The rest of the United States funded television and school campaigns from the $206 billion settlement, which were never implemented by the state of South Carolina. The budget got hit by a bus. And Rage lives on.

"I think it got stuck in our hearts."

Cris Ivan – Rage Viralmentalist #11

But it doesn't stop there in the results category. As Viralmentalist #11 Chris Ivan puts it:

Rage made a difference in our lives; and I hope that it made a difference in our communities as well. I see RAGE a little bit differently today than I did five years ago. I think what I was missing then was the underlying

power of what we were doing. It's not that we enraged
people to get out in the streets on an everyday basis,
I think it got stuck in our hearts.

Yes, Rage is about teens in South Carolina. It was and is a
movement to give them a voice. But the lessons learned have
fueled the growth of a 360-year-old tool company. And sparked
one of the largest retailers in the nation to say, "Why can't we
give a voice and a platform to our passionate musical instrument
employees and customers?" So we ask you this: How do you measure
changing someone's life?

We started the Fiskars movement in four specific cities. One
of our goals was to increase sales 10 percent within the first nine
months. Our online aim was to increase mentions of the brand on
the Internet—beyond the Fiskateer site—by at least 10 percent.

According to the company's sales data, the Fiskateer movement
doubled sales in the cities where we started as compared with
cities with the same sales trends that had no Fiskateer presence.
When we again tracked online references to the brand, we found
that they increased 240 percent within the first four months. To
date, they've increased more than 600 percent.

But it doesn't stop there with the Fiskateers, either.

Fiskateers are doing their own marketing and creating their
own messages: T-shirts, bumper stickers, business cards, and
RACs (random acts of crafting) in public spaces, all in the name
of Fiskars. The list goes on and on. And again, instead of being
the logo police and squashing those efforts, Fiskars supports and
encourages them, which fuels the fire of the initiative.

Another way we measure this movement's success is by analyzing how the Fiskateer community contributes across many
different departments within the company. And this translates
to the things that they *don't* have to spend money on.

For example, Fiskars's R&D department has a direct line
into members of the community, who now choose the names

and colors for new products. An engineer can set up a chat or reach out to individual Fiskateers by name and reputation to gather their input and opinions. This reduces costs for focus groups and research, because the community's hand-raisers are willing and eager to share their thoughts on any particular subject. On average, R&D receives 13 new ideas for products per month—for free. Some of these get developed and produced. So Fiskateers go to the store and see a product that they had a part in developing, testing, or naming—and that good old feeling of ownership ensues.

Because Fiskateers are out there actively talking about Fiskars and its products on other web sites, blogs, and message boards, Fiskars spends less money for online ad placements. This is also true for Fiskateers who answer people's concerns and questions about Fiskars products. If someone posts a question online about a problem with a product, Fiskateers are able to respond before anyone from corporate can find it and answer. Jay Gillespie explains:

> If we have a product problem at midnight online, this group of 7,000 will jump in there and solve problems for us. They're integrated into customer service, [and] engaged in research and development. Our product managers are in conversations with them. It's really an incredible asset.

In other words, this company has a community of over 7,000 individuals who know how to troubleshoot and are more than willing to share that knowledge. On top of these things, Fiskateers show up and take care of potentially nightmarish public relations issues before the company can even prepare a formal response. Fiskateers are defenders of the brand.

By conservative estimates—because the community is playing so many roles in so many different departments—there is about a 500 percent yearly return on the value of community compared with what Fiskars spends on it. So they don't just measure the money they're making; they also measure the money they're *saving* and can therefore use for other things.

In the case of Best Buy's Mi11 musical instruments movement, it's too early to tell about sales results. What we do know is that engagement is running deep. For example, 12 percent of the employees in the musical instruments division applied for the leadership positions. That's unheard of for a giant retail brand like Best Buy—considering the fact that a lot of those stores-within-stores were open only a couple of months at the time. Of course, there are many other things that will be measured. Best Buy Marketing Strategy and Communication executive Jamie Plesser weighs in: "A movement will help us land the awareness challenge. It helps us deliver on credibility. A conversation is an experience in and of itself."

> "A conversation is an experience in and of itself."
>
> Jamie Plesser – Best Buy
> Marketing Strategy and Communication

So open up your mind to results. Yes, we live in a world where movements need to be justified because they show up on a profit-and-loss report as a line item. Make no mistake about it, those results need to be tied to dollar signs. But *in addition* to that, think about the other ways a movement can be measured. And to be completely honest, some of it can't be tied to dollars. Like the story of the Fiskateers donating crafting supplies to a fellow community member whose house burned down. Or the Fiskateer who offered to be tested as a possible match when another community member found out her father needed a kidney transplant. Measure that in dollars, if you can.

As we stated in the beginning of this book, the true test of a movement's success is to create something so powerful—so meaningful—that your advocates don't want to live without it. So if your budget gets slashed, they will pick up the banner and march forward without you. That can't be quantified on a piece of paper. But the by-products of it can.

So find the passion conversation.

Start with the first conversation.

Look for inspirational leadership.

Create a barrier of entry.

Empower your fans with knowledge.

Make sure you integrate shared ownership into your movement.

Build it on a powerful identity.

Tie online and off-line efforts and tactics together.

Make those fans of yours feel like rock stars.

And . . .

BONUS LESSON: MOVEMENTS FIGHT AN INJUSTICE

Yes, movements fight an injustice in the world. It's straightforward to see that for organizations like Love146, where the injustice lies in the horrors of child-sex slavery and exploitation. Martin Luther King Jr. fought against the injustice of inequality. That's easy to identify, too. But what is your injustice? You might think it's hard to find, but it lies in those passion conversations you have while you're collecting insights and encouraging participation.

The injustice for Fiskars was the nastiness on other crafting message boards. Because of this, they ignited a movement that celebrated crafting of all kinds from people of various skill levels with different backgrounds and beliefs—all in a safe environment.

The injustice for IndieBound and the American Booksellers Association was the homogenization of selling books in America through the Amazons and Barnes & Nobles. So they ignited a movement that celebrated the independence of those individuals who were brave enough to put a stake in the ground and contribute to their neighborhoods' uniqueness.

The Park Angels' injustice was the deterioration of the public spaces in a city proud of its history. Rage against the Haze's injustice was the tobacco industry's manipulation of teens and South Carolina's apathy to do anything about it.

Even a giant company like Best Buy can fight injustices. Theirs was the intimidating, daunting task of going into a musical instrument store and looking at that guitar or drum set. So they proved that you can sell premium brands in an environment that could celebrate and get excited about the magic associated with playing and creating music for all skill levels.

So what's your injustice? Dig. You'll find it. And when you do, don't let go. Cling to it with all you've got. Because that is your purpose and your guiding light. And without it, you have a marketing program—not a movement.

Remember: Movements move toward a goal that transcends putting money in your pocket. You might think it's cheesy, but movements change lives on several levels. And there's no reason you can't change your customers' lives for the better, whether you're out to end one of the most horrific things on the planet like the kidnapping and exploitation of kids, or you're using an orange-handled scissor to unite and celebrate people's love of crafting.

This book started by pointing out how marketers are beginning to shy away from the word *campaign* and are beginning to adopt and use new words like *movements*. But take heed in this warning: If it doesn't have all of the elements on the list, then it's not a movement. It's a campaign in sheep's clothing. And you might be able to fool a lot of the people out there, but you can't fool those who are already drawn to you. So don't even try.

Now is the time to build something that will last as long as your customers want it to. And the only way to do that is to involve them from the beginning. Movements move people to action. Movements transform companies. Movements change lives. If you're a company whose sole reason for existence is to make money, we're sad for you. Why not change your corner of the world for the better? Why not save the day for your fans? Why not start a movement and be a part of something bigger than yourself?

Now all you have to do is roll up your sleeves and get to work.

Your Turn

Igniting movements is hard work.

It's building with people, not just tools.

Our belief is simple . . . we're all in marketing grad school. We're not experts. Frankly there are no experts yet. And that's why we're all in this together.

There are more lessons to learn, more stories to share and more movements to ignite . . .

So, join the Brains on Fire movement at www.brainsonfireblog .com. Let's write the next chapters *together*.

This is the beginning, not the end.

About the Authors

ROBBIN PHILLIPS

 I'm known as the Courageous President around the halls of Brains on Fire. (Wait, we don't have halls.) I love my two kids in a way words can't explain. I've worked with brands such as BMW, Colonial Williamsburg Foundation, Love146, and Ryobi Tools. I love hot yoga, cold beer, sunny days and starry nights. I believe writing inspires thinking. I write and think out loud at brainsonfire. com/blog. I think everyone works better when they are having fun. I expect my business dealings to be profitable. I want to create positive change in the world. I am pretty psyched PQ Media named us one of the top three word of mouth companies in the industry in 2007. And that Wommie Award was cool. (Yahoo! and Coca-Cola got one along with us.) I believe love is a circular transaction. I try really hard to keep things simple. Some days I am better at that than others. I am part of the Brains on Fire Movement.

GREG CORDELL

I'm Chief Inspiration Officer at Brains on Fire. I work for my children. I've been an inventor, a writer, a designer, a choreographer, a composer . . . In another life, I might be a philosopher. I believe all people are brilliant. I drive American. I've spoken at AIGA gatherings, PRSA conferences, corporate events, and the happy hour around the corner. Because I like to talk. I cry, too—at weddings and animated movies. I've worked on creative solutions for Yakima, BMW, Don Pablo's Mexican Restaurants, Applebee's and Best Buy. I've had work used as the backdrop for an American President's war on drugs. I've added crazy-big numbers to national brands' bottom lines. I like being a conduit for inspirational energy. I believe everybody deserves to be excited about something. I believe there is always a better way and the greatest thing people can experience is to realize they need each other.

GENO CHURCH

My title on the Brains on Fire web site is Word of Mouth Inspiration Officer, but I consider myself more of a Pathfinder for our clients and Brains on Fire. And I've been down that path with Fiskars Brands, Best Buy, Colonial Williamsburg, the American Booksellers Association, Charleston Parks Conservancy, the U.S. Office of National Drug Control Policy, Love146 and Rage Against the Haze (South Carolina's youth led anti-tobacco movement). I wouldn't be here without a ton of support and love from my family at home and the Brains on Fire family. I'm lucky to be an explorer in conversations. I like uncovering the DNA of sustainable word of mouth movements and building them from the ground up. I'm a blogger. I'm a talker—at places like the Word of Mouth Marketing Association, the Public Relations Society of America, American Marketing Association, the New Comm Research Communications Forum, and the World Africa Customer Management Conference. I used to play in a glam-rock band. I survived.

Spike Jones is a writer and editor who gave our message one voice. He is currently SVP of Digital at Fleishman-Hillard. You can find him over at www.askspike.com.

Index

INDEX